BEING
COWLITZ

BEING COWLITZ

HOW ONE TRIBE RENEWED AND

SUSTAINED ITS IDENTITY

Christine Dupres

UNIVERSITY OF
WASHINGTON PRESS
Seattle & London

© 2014 by the University of Washington Press
Printed and bound in the United States of America
Composed in Chaparral, a typeface designed by Carol Twombly
Design by Dustin Kilgore
17 16 15 14   5 4 3 2 1

All rights reserved. No part of this publication may be reproduced or transmitted in any form or by any means, electronic or mechanical, including photocopy, recording, or any information storage or retrieval system, without permission in writing from the publisher.

University of Washington Press
www.washington.edu/uwpress

Library of Congress Cataloging-in-Publication Data

Dupres, Christine Joy.
Being Cowlitz : how one tribe renewed and sustained its identity / Christine Joy Dupres.
    pages cm
ncludes bibliographical references and index.
ISBN 978-0-295-99396-6 (hardcover : acid-free paper) 1. Cowlitz Indian Tribe, Washington—History. 2. Cowlitz Indians—History. 3. Cowlitz Indians—Ethnic identity. 4. Cowlitz Indians—Social life and customs. 5. Cowlitz Indians—Folklore. I. Title.
E99.C877D87 2014
979.7004'97943—dc23
              2014020291

The paper used in this publication is acid-free and meets the minimum requirements of American National Standard for Information Sciences Permanence of Paper for Printed Library Materials, ANSI Z39.48–1984.∞

CONTENTS

Acknowledgments vii

1. Introduction 3

2. Cowlitz History 14

3. Historical Discourse and the Use
of Landscape: Genres of Attachment 32

Image Gallery 71

4. The Importance of Leaders and Legends 81

5. The Importance of Personal History Narrative 107

6. The Importance of Personal History Narrative in
Shaping Oral History and Myth 124

Bibliography 148

ACKNOWLEDGMENTS

With love to my family: Creon, Shea, Chai, and Chelsea. You are the center of my world.

With gratitude to my family and friends, whose encouragement and unflagging faith have seen me through this project.

Love always to my mother and grandmothers, for the prickly summers spent in a berry patch.

Special thanks to my editor and friend, Michael Ward. Thick and thin and through it all, this book has strengthened our friendship.

And finally, with admiration to the Cowlitz tribal people, and all among them who dare history. We remember the Cowlitz elders passed, and await the children to come.

Always remember, always.

BEING COWLITZ

CHAPTER 1

Introduction

EVERYONE HAS A STORY. THIS STORY IS BOTH MINE AND THAT OF others: the members of my family and of my tribe, the Cowlitz. This is a story about stories too, about how people use stories to define for themselves who they are. This story is partially mine, partially theirs.

This book began as a hunt for stories, a personal journey to discover the lost songs and histories of my Indian ancestors—my aunts and grandmothers of the Cowlitz Tribe. Along the way, I realized that these stories were not just my aunts' and grandmothers' stories, but the stories of the Cowlitz Indians themselves. In uncovering these stories, I was finding the identity of a tribe that had been scattered across various states, a tribe without a land, a tribe whose sense of identity was in constant danger of dissolving into the blankness of unrecorded history. This search took me to various reservations in Washington State, to mossy cemeteries amid the northwest pine, and to the living room of a dying linguist in Canada. This quest made me a few very good friends among the Cowlitz; it got me, by an odd twist of fate, an administrative job and an election to tribal council. The search had me wandering to museums and falling in love with my grandmothers. I fell in love with my own past as well. The hunt for these stories also taught me how to create some distance from the romance of my Native heritage, a distance necessary to fully understand the answers to the questions I was asking. Ultimately, the exploration of these Cowlitz stories brought me to a deeper understanding of what the inheritance of this history really means.

I always had questions about where I came from, but they became more urgent in the early 1990s when I, then a young mom of twins and a new graduate student at the University of Oregon, began studying eighteenth-century English literature and twentieth-century feminist theater. This is when the journey really began for me. This is where I start my story. In 1994, early into my graduate studies, I befriended Andy, a Siletz Indian man. He seemed to have a handle on being Indian, despite (or perhaps because of) his flaxen hair and ice-blue eyes. He was connected—personally, socially, and politically (as a formal member)—to the Siletz Tribe. This foundational identity was for Andy a launching point for much that he accomplished (and for many whom he alienated) during his graduate tenure. Andy talked the talk and was willing to stand on principle when he felt that academic practices and policy at the university were racist. He also walked the walk, ensuring that he kept up Native practices and ceremony.

In contrast, I felt that I was pretty bad at being an Indian. I knew that I had Native blood. I had always been told that I was Indian (Cowlitz and Cree), and my Grandma lived on the Siletz Reservation near my hometown of Newport, Oregon. Still, my mother had not taken the time to demonstrate what "being an Indian" meant, though later I would come to understand how she lived. This knowledge would help me understand what it means to live as a Native woman, realizing how deeply Native culture was embedded in us both. My mother was not active in the political realm of the Cowlitz Tribe. She seldom took me to Cowlitz General Council meetings (as her mother had taken her). Although my grandmother had made sure that her children were enrolled in the Cowlitz Tribe, my mother had not enrolled my sibling and me. In my early twenties, I took it upon myself to call the tribal office for paperwork and completed my genealogy and application for membership. I applied to be a citizen of the Cowlitz Tribe in 1989 and my acceptance came in 1990.

It was in this context that Andy and I had a long talk one day. I confessed to him how timid and awkward I felt about "being" a Cowlitz/Cree woman. I wondered aloud how I could know, definitively, that I was a Native person. "Well, what is it for *you*?" he asked me. "Why are you drawn to your tribe and people?" I answered, simply, "I feel pulled to remember." With that Andy smiled. If I was drawn to figure out my place among a people and felt a pull to remember, he said, then I was definitely an Indian. Of sorts. It was this "of sorts" that made me start looking into my heritage.

This is what I found: In 1841 my Cree ancestors came to the Cowlitz Prairie in the Washington Territory. They were voyageurs, fur transporters, in the employ of the Hudson's Bay Company, and traveled to the prairie from the Red River area of Manitoba, Canada, down into the Washington Territory to seek trade and work. They quickly settled in and intermarried with the Cowlitz people. One of these was my Cowlitz ancestor Lucy Skloutwout, or Hakire. The Cowlitz people accepted the Cree voyageurs as kin. My great grandmother, Rose, spoke French Cree and was able to speak Lower Cowlitz. French Cree was her first language, the only language her father spoke. Thus my family—like so many Native families—was a mix of tribes, just as this book explores a mix of histories, my own Cowlitz ancestry and the history of the Cowlitz Tribe itself. Both histories are closely entwined. My intellectual journey thus began with a personal one, with the need to figure out for myself, for my mom, and for my grandmothers what it meant to be Cowlitz and Cree, and how we all belonged.

Because the Cowlitz Tribe for years had no land base or reservation, its people are scattered over southwestern Washington and other areas of the United States. The Cowlitz General Council—held twice annually—provides an important venue for gathering and communication. I started going regularly to these meetings, where I became interested in matters of voice and authority. I started paying attention to whose voice was heard, whose story was ultimately being told, and how these stories—and these storytellers—shaped, for me and for the others present at Council meetings, both personal and tribal identity. It was then that I made a discovery of a different kind: I knew what the focus of my graduate work would be. I would write a dissertation analyzing how the Cowlitz leaders articulate and understand themselves and their history, and how through their authority, these tribal leaders bring this understanding of themselves as a people to the Cowlitz group as a whole. I took notes, watching how the leaders used different rhetorical strategies to demonstrate tribal priorities. I wondered what these strategies tell us about group making and identity, especially when the group itself is under a quiet but constant threat of dissolution.

The Cowlitz people have endured and (continue to) surmount the forces of erasure that is common to all the tribes in the United States: fatal disease; removal from their land due to pressure to move or sell through economic necessity; and cultural loss created as a result of cooperation with the dominant culture, which was often racist in policy if not deportment. Given these pressures, one way the Cowlitz could articulate and maintain their identity was by defining themselves as different from the prevailing (white) culture. They did this, in part, by maintaining an attachment to their land and through a reliance on their leadership—a leadership that has engaged the federal government at every critical turn and that has carefully marked and rehearsed Cowlitz collective memory.

This attempt at attachment to the land is especially important for the Cowlitz Tribe, who, though it has tribal sites in Longview and Toledo, both in Washington State, as yet has no formal land base or reservation. The people, though concentrated in southwestern Washington, are scattered over other areas in the United States. Because of this lack of centrality, the Cowlitz General Council holds important opportunities for gathering and communication. I have been attending these meetings since 1995. The first I attended were emotionally overwhelming for me. There I sat, among almost two hundred Cowlitz people, many of whom resembled me, right down to the round and tea-colored eyes. I heard the council chairman, John Barnett, speak of the trials of his people, *my* people, and how they prevailed. I saw history alive, on that modest stage. I saw the old ones sit quietly. I saw ceremony and heard voices raised in common.

As a graduate student, I was inclined to turn first to books for what I needed, but books can only do so much. Quiet myths upon a page cannot live in the way that a myth spoken in context can. I listened carefully to spiritual elder Roy Wilson as he told stories of Coyote, of the Deer Sisters, and of other mythical figures. A young woman both curious and impressionable, I listened to the leaders talk and watched the long panel of tribal council members who sat before me. Intellectually, I understood the complications of my position as a woman of European and Native American descent. I understood the complexities of racial and ethnic identity. I understood the implications of claiming space and place as one's own. I understood, yet as I sat at the Cowlitz General Council I felt completely, totally at home. Watching Chairman Barnett and Roy Wilson lead the proceedings, I became captivated by their articulations of Native identity that existed alongside the more formal articulations of Native identity stemming from anthropological research, legal engagement, and academic scholarship. Throughout the mid-1990s, I became more and more involved in my relationship with and my research of the Cowlitz Tribe. I used all means at my disposal: I conducted interviews with elders, whose yield was mysterious to me; I read outdated copies of the Cowlitz *Yooyoolah* newsletters and old news clippings from defunct papers; I tracked down records from cemeteries and other data gleaned from archives. By attending meetings and taking notes on my observations of the tribal leaders whose command and confidence inspired me, I was forming and strengthening my Native identity. I was performing a personal repatriation.

This project of discovery began not so much with a concern for cultural renaissance as with my need to hear the stories of the elders and the mythology of the tribe. What, I wondered, was our inheritance? What did we tell each other? And why? These questions refined themselves as I immersed myself deeper into the ethnological scholarship of the tribes of the Pacific Northwest and their tribal politics. I listened to Cowlitz leaders, and through their guidance and shared knowledge, I began to make sense of the political struggle that lay at the heart of Cowlitz history and identity. I began to question the way in which Cowlitz tribal people, especially the tribal leaders, understood themselves as enduring: enduring against the constraints of the government; against the passing of time; against erosion; against all odds, since "time immemorial," as one tribal member put it. My focus eventually narrowed to the contemporary response to the historical pressures created by the Cowlitz people's relationship to their own history.

This history occurred in relationship to the federal government (through cooperation with its mandates and processes) as well as in other, more somber places: as a fragmentary memory of an elder's story or a last Sahaptin word whispered. What, I would ask the leaders repeatedly, did the leaders seem to know that taught them what it meant to be Cowlitz? Was it the stories learned at the knees of elders some seventy years ago at council meetings, or was it the education gained by traveling to Washington, D.C., to deal with the U.S. Congress and select political committees? Was it about the times spent in the woods or at the medicine wheel, or the time spent pacing before a senator's closed door? Was identity characterized by a pilgrimage to the Yakama Reservation to see relatives, or an election to tribal government? I wondered how others in the tribe came to a tribal identity, a tribal lineage, such as mine. Where, I wondered, did they get these understandings? What did they know about their ancestors, both white and Indian? Why did some individuals—when multiracial and multicultural like me—choose to identify with their Native heritage rather than their other one (or ones)? Was this identification exclusive or more generalized? Did they also want to know about their German grandfather, for example?

As I learned more about the Cowlitz Tribe, I began to filter my own experience through this new information, and I discovered that what I had been raised to do by my mother and grandmothers seemed to be rooted in their learned experience—an experience shared with other Cowlitz and Cree people, consisting of cultural practices transmitted informally over time. There was certainly a case to make for Native identity existing in the motions of my life, for my many summers spent in the Cascade Mountains picking berries or digging clams and harvesting mussels by the Pacific Ocean. Though my working-class parents lived quite comfortably, our trips to the grocery store were only slightly more common than our forest trips that yielded a harvest of venison and berries or our catch of shellfish and salmon from the sea. I was eager to claim the motions of my everyday life as Native. The way I was raised was inherently the way of an indigenous people who lived by the seasons and land's bounty: digging, clamming, picking seasonal berries, fishing and hunting, and, as my mother always said, "putting things by."

In 1998, I began my research on the Cowlitz Tribe in earnest. I keep close contact with a number of people from the tribe, many of whom are friends or family and some of whom I interviewed for my dissertation. Through email, phone, formal recorded interviews, observation, and numerous conversations, I conducted fieldwork with sixteen members of the tribe. These individuals ranged in age from their early twenties to early eighties and all lived in Washington State, from the Puget Sound area down to Vancouver, Washington, near the Columbia River. While everyone I interviewed inspired me and helped shape my experience and knowledge of Cowlitz culture, I eventually chose to focus my analysis primarily on John Barnett and Roy Wilson, two prominent Cowlitz leaders. The emphasis further narrowed to their rhetorical and leadership styles within the key venue of Cowlitz General Council meetings, where a good deal of explication regarding what it means to be a Cowlitz could be garnered through their narratives and performances. In this book I share the insights gained from listening and talking to these two men. I still think that the best way to understand what makes a tribe a tribe is by studying the stories its people tell. These two men tell some of the best stories.[1]

Cowlitz chairman John Barnett and spiritual elder Roy Wilson have served politically for the tribe for many years and are prominent, vocal men. In formal interviews over a number of years, I arranged my questions to elicit personal histories. I looked closely at what John Barnett, Roy Wilson, and other interviewees chose to tell me, noticing especially that what they had to say was often less personal than collective and historical. I was struck by particular narrative and rhetorical strategies that emerged in conversations with each leader. Examples include John's mention of the Treaty of Olympia or *United States v. Mitchell et al.*, a U.S. Supreme Court case he was involved in as an allottee, and his use of humor and frequent reference to the natural world as a metaphor for the Cowlitz people's persistence and predicament. I noticed Roy's emphasis on spiritual renewal through demonstration of Methodist and pan-Indian religious practice as well as his passion to tell anew the stories and myths he had heard and read about the Cowlitz people. Roy's personal experience narratives inevitably referred back to historical and social processes within the Cowlitz Tribe. I asked each man what it was he wanted the Cowlitz people to remember. Neither man took too much time to talk about his personal achievements, describing instead the Cowlitz people's endurance, success, and survival against all odds. I became particularly interested in contemporary Cowlitz creative and aesthetic life and how it relates to tribal identity and cultural continuity.

Another reason I focused on these oral narratives, aside from their intrinsic value as examples of identity creation and the motives behind it, was that I could not rely on primary source material alone to create a history of the tribe. Much of the material on the Cowlitz Indians is scattered, incomplete, or difficult to summarize. Online and in repositories at the Catholic Archdiocese in Seattle are Catholic Church records and cemetery records for sites around the Cowlitz Tribe's usual and accustomed territory. There are also repositories of Cowlitz materials and information in local historical societies (in Washington State's Lewis and Cowlitz Counties, for example).

Local newspapers in such Washington cities as Longview, Chehalis, and Centralia have long occupied themselves with Cowlitz business but in no systematic way. Even from 1911, public commentary seemed to be amused by the political attempts of the Cowlitz people.

More recently, in-depth information about the Cowlitz in print form is difficult to find with the exception of a plenitude of "gray literature"—archival documents from governmental personnel (and correspondence files of such personnel) and such lay persons as early pioneers, explorers, and missionaries. The literature is called "gray" because it is difficult to acquire through traditional channels. This material is tricky to use, however, because often, especially in early settlement accounts, it functioned as a reinforcement of the colonial agenda or as anti-Indian sentiment. This material thus tends to reveal more about the biases of its authors than about the Indians themselves; early pioneer reminiscences, in fashion throughout the late-nineteenth and early-twentieth centuries, provided insight into the sorts of romanticization and chauvinism Cowlitz and other Indians endured at the hands of settlers. So-called gray literature could be informative and might well document historical fact in that it tracks specific verifiable instances in time, yet it offers little regarding Cowlitz priorities for naming and belonging. Instead, it imposed external, non-Native means for comprehending the Cowlitz people.

Despite the problems of primary documentation on the subject, I have used certain conceptual methods of folklore as a solid ground for the consideration of some important questions. Folklore—especially folklore that focuses on performance—has since the mid-1960s given us detailed, well-theorized accounts of Native American performance and narrative. Folklorists have come to realize that concepts of "group" and "belonging," especially as they are shared through performance, have significant force in keeping people together despite their differences. For the Cowlitz the most important concepts that help solidify their tribal identity are those of land, corporate anger (anger of the people, the corpus), group persistence against all odds, and familial survival. In the Cowlitz community, although the meaning and function of these critical concepts changes from member to member, they remain a common theme among the majority of people I interviewed, from both general tribal membership as well as tribal leadership. Many Cowlitz people take pride in their survival as a people, claiming that the tribe will overcome governmental obstacles through their stubbornness and perseverance.

Another common comment among those interviewed was that they feel most attached to their Cowlitz ancestry when surrounded by nature. Said tribal council member Robin Torner (2005, 2): "When I am out in the forests alone, it's just me and the woods as they were before the settlers turned hunting—a noble, necessary function of life—into a perverted blood sport." I even found such notions in my own family: for instance, my mother will always bring up the importance of her Cowlitz ancestry to make a point about filial piety in the modern day. If I was being lazy, I would surely hear something like: "Our [Cowlitz] grandmother was a tough old Indian who worked every day of her life." Or, in regard to my sibling, she might say: "Your brother and you share the same blood. You should never quarrel." Or, of her Cowlitz ancestry, she might tell me: "They have never stopped [in their efforts at recognition], not since I can remember" (Jamtgaard 2003).

Although folklore is the theoretical lens I use the most throughout this analysis, I also sought out recent studies by scholars Alexandra Harmon (2008 and 1998), Jon Daehnke (2013 and 2010), and others who write about the dynamics of cultural identity among Native Americans of the Pacific Northwest. Harmon and Daehnke's work is particularly useful because their scholarship overlaps ethnogeographically and chronologically with my own. We have a shared interest in the contested and dynamic meanings of Native identity, orality, and performance, as well as the symbolic uses and contested meanings of sites of history. These scholars and I also share an interest in how memory functions in a group and how it can be held in common and in place (Daehnke 2013, 39). Harmon's treatment of the Isaac Stevens treaties of 1855, as seen in *Broken Promises* (1998) and *Indians in the Making* (2008), is a case in point. In *Broken Promises,* Harmon (2008, 9) makes a compelling argument that the Stevens treaties and their effects were so uniform and so wide-reaching that when assessing their impact, we should "consider the document and its ... effects in common." Daehnke works with the Chinook, whose history and relationship to the federal government parallels that of the Cowlitz. The Chinook received federal recognition by the Clinton administration on January 3, 2001, but the Bush administration removed it on July 5, 2002, because of objections made by the Quinault. The Chinook and the Cowlitz have shared the same territory and have intermarried for centuries, yet in modern times, as Daehnke (2013, 45) writes in his article about the building of the Cathlapotle Longhouse, they have occasionally been at odds over sites of heritage and how those sites are interpreted.

Harmon and Daehnke share my belief that a shared system of constructing relationships with outsiders (such as is required by the Cowlitz leaders) requires a keen consideration of power relations. Such a relationship is far more complex than official histories have led us to believe. There has been very little written about the Cowlitz, and essentially nothing written of their performance of myth, biography, legend, and landscape ("landscape" refers to a kind of performance elicited through use of these other three methods). I hope to (at least partially) fill the gap created by this paucity of investigation into Cowlitz methods of identity creation. As a Cowlitz woman myself, my presence is a key part of my methodology and investigation.

My personal understanding of the Cowlitz people and their various performances, and my means of conducting and interpreting the information collected, both inform and complicate my observations in ways that nontribal members would not experience. I am not unique in my situation as a younger Cowlitz woman looking to identify and make meaning within the Cowlitz whole, yet as a researcher and writer, I am quite unique in my status within the tribe. I am both inside it, looking at myself, and outside it, looking at them. Of course, insiders are outsiders at various times too, so perhaps my status is not as different as I might think. I may occupy the table as a Cowlitz Council member, hence alienating a tribal friend who does not trust tribal politics or politicians; I may be seen as an upstart by those who have held tribal positions, membership, or office longer than I have. I may be distanced from elders by the difference in our age, experience, or other circumstances. I may likewise be distanced from those who are differently educated.

As a folklorist and ethnographer, I have certain means to consider the rhetorical practices of the tribal council, but then again my "distance" from the tribal council, and by extension my impartiality, is arguable given that

I am also a member of tribal politics. At any given time, I am neither within the tribal community nor without it, never solidly impartial in my privilege as a tribal observer. The model I establish here might well subject me to all the problems and critical analyses of the thing I set out to analyze. In the interest of clarity, both academic and personal, my "agenda" as it were must be made apparent to the reader. How does my experience, the experience of the individual, speak to the experience of the group as a whole? Are the priorities I set forth here more urgent, more pressing, more reflective of the Cowlitz as a whole than other priorities? Does this lend heft and insight to my argument, or make it suspect? As it is clear that I am not a detached observer, I at times have written myself into this text. I want a way to explain how there is a simultaneous and internal "tribal making" that goes on within the individuals of the Cowlitz Indian Tribe as they (we) negotiate issues of race, culture, and acculturation, and that addresses the issues of where they (we), as legally identified and self-identified Cowlitz individuals, create meaning and continuity.

And so, with all that said, let us now begin to learn about the Cowlitz Indian tribe.

---

[1] Some might wonder at the relatively small size of my interview pool. Because I chose tribal council members and political leaders as a focus, the majority of my interviews were with politicians of the Cowlitz Tribe. There are roughly two dozen politicians, and more than half of my interviews involved these people, which is a good representative sample.

CHAPTER 2

Cowlitz History

> Five centuries of survival under the most excruciating pressure of killing diseases, wars, land expropriation and official government policy–forced assimilation, then outright termination. Yet the tribes are now the strongest they have been in a century and a half. Never has this land seen such staying power.
>
> CHARLES F. WILKINSON

WHO ARE THE COWLITZ? WHERE DO THEY COME FROM? ARE THEY indeed now stronger than before? What would the Cowlitz themselves say about their own staying power? Through interviews and observation, I feel that by and large the Cowlitz people perceive themselves to be acculturated but not assimilated. One cultural leader signs his correspondences with the word "unconquered," which captures the essence of the general attitude of the Cowlitz. Although "acculturation" and "assimilation" share qualitative similarities, they are not interchangeable terms. The Cowlitz have assumed many of the majority culture's practices and norms, but they have also managed to remain a distinct society despite these adaptations. To say that the Cowlitz have been assimilated would be to suggest that they have been absorbed by the dominant culture; this is simply not true. Cowlitz members generally feel that they have not "given up," which to them means that they have not "assimilated." They still feel distinctly Cowlitz and identify as such—despite not speaking Salish or Taidnapam, despite a loss of usual and accustomed territory (save for Saint Mary's and Longview), and despite a discontinuity in their daily work as it relates to lives once lived on the land. Not only do Cowlitz chair John Barnett and spiritual leader Roy Wilson not think of themselves as assimilated, they also are deeply committed to an expression and continuation of cultural and political practices. This, despite the fact that the tribe does not have a federally recognized reservation.

The Cowlitz Tribe, numbering about forty-two hundred members today, is growing in enrollment because incentives for tribal membership have increased since the tribe won federal recognition in January 2002. The members of the tribe, living principally in western Washington State, are descendents of an aboriginal people estimated to have inhabited the Cowlitz River region for fifty-five hundred to seven thousand years, right up until the twentieth century. Their territory ranged from the Columbia River to the Puget Sound and eastward to the foothills of the Cascade Mountains. A number of Cowlitz lived further south and east, on the Lewis River, roughly between the famous Mount Saint Helens and its quieter companion, Mount Adams. They lived as far south as Sauvie Island, on the Columbia River, and at a town now called Battle Ground, Washington, so named for Cowlitz Chief Umtuch, who was killed in mysterious circumstances during the Indian Wars of 1855. It is likely that in aboriginal times, before white settlement, disease, and dislocation, the Cowlitz ranged further still.

Before the arrival of European traders and explorers in the late eighteenth century, as many as two hundred thousand Native Americans inhabited the Northwest Coast area, making it one of the most densely populated nonagricultural areas in the world. Northwest Coast Indians experienced European and other contact relatively late compared with other indigenous peoples in other parts of the United States, especially in the Northeast. Northwest Coast Indians first encountered the Europeans (Spaniards, French Canadian fur traders like my ancestors, British, and Americans) in the late eighteenth century. The earliest written recording of the Cowlitz is usually attributed to explorers Meriwether Lewis and William Clark. When their expedition passed the "Coweliskee" River, the explorers made mention of the Indians living there. In his unpublished manuscript "Cowlitz Chronicles," Cowlitz member Robin Torner (1994) notes an interesting incident, recorded by the anthropologist Franz Boas in *Chinook Texts* (1894), regarding a series of shipwrecks that occurred between 1700 and 1750. Torner (1994,7) writes that around 1750:

> Several shipwrecks occurred on the Washington and Oregon coasts, near the mouth of the Columbia [and] word of [one] wreck and two men with "faces like bears" spread up the river and coast and many tribes sent representatives down to investigate. Boas says Quinault, Chehalis, Cowlitz and Klikitat all came to see for themselves. The incident Boas describes may be the first written record of any Cowlitz person encountering a European. The sailors could easily have been American, Spanish, Dutch, Russian, French or English, as all these nations had trading coasts at this time and full beards, "faces like bears," were common.

Cowlitz historian Judith Irwin (1979 and 1994) has discovered an early written record concerning the Cowlitz people: a citation by the employees of the Pacific Fur Company who were met by a fleet of Cowlitz canoes as they paddled up the Cowlitz River in 1811. Washington Territory was active with trade, and from the early 1800s well into the 1840s the Cowlitz had numerous encounters and dealings with the Hudson's Bay Company, the Pacific Fur Company, the North West Company, and explorers in the area, including artist Paul Kane, who visited the Cowlitz in the winter of 1846.

Within a hundred years after initial contact with Europeans, the aboriginal population of Pacific Northwest tribes had declined more than 80 percent. Devastation by disease was especially extreme in the 1830s and 1840s. Some Native populations fell by over 92 percent, largely because of such diseases as smallpox and syphilis. The population decline created profound cultural and psychological dislocation for all the Native peoples along the Northwest Coast, among them the Cowlitz, who lost upward of 80 percent of their people because of disease. This included intermittent fever, an ailment now speculated to be a form of flu that began in the late 1820s, followed by measles in 1848, and a smallpox epidemic in 1853. This catastrophic and rapid loss of lives had a devastating effect on kinship systems and irrevocably altered Native cultural, spiritual, and material ways of life.

It was during the 1830s that the powerful Hudson's Bay Company subsidiary, the Puget Sound Agricultural Company, established itself on the

Cowlitz Prairie to raise crops and livestock that would feed the Russian American Company employees in Alaska. Catholic missionaries would settle the same area. Fathers Francois Norbert Blanchet and Modeste Demers arrived in 1838 and worked with varying degrees of success to convert the Cowlitz and other Indians in the area to Catholicism. The Organic Act created Oregon Territory in 1848 and Washington Territory on March 2, 1853, which brought an encroachment of white settlers into Indian lands, causing much discontent among the Native inhabitants. The Donation Land Claim Act, passed as law in September 1850, promised 320 acres of land to single men and 640 acres to married couples who settled Oregon Territory before the end of 1850. Half that acreage was given to those who lay claim before 1854. This act, coupled with the Treaty of Washington in 1846, profoundly altered Indian life in the Pacific Northwest. Over a five-year span the small but substantial number of white settlers in Oregon Territory grew by thousands.

By the late nineteenth century, the Native Americans of western Washington and the wider Northwest Coast either succumbed to or were attenuated by the federal government's systematic and highly effective effort to move them from their Native lands to alien and often desolate reservation lands. In 1855 numerous conflicts arose between territorial settlers and the Natives of the Northwest, especially in eastern Washington, where the strife between prospectors and Natives was keen. The Cowlitz, however, did not engage in the Indian Wars of 1855, wars that resulted in numerous treaties and displacements onto reservations for the treaty-signing tribes; for this reason, among others, they are historically regarded as having excellent relationships with their European neighbors.

The Cowlitz never negotiated a formal treaty, but they were approached by Washington Territorial Governor Isaac Stevens in the late winter of 1855 in the town that is now Cosmopolis, Washington. From February 25 through March 3 of that year, Stevens negotiated with the tribes. The Cowlitz firmly denied his request to leave their prairie homelands and join their sometime enemy, the Quinault, on land much further north, nearer to the sea and thickly forested. The historical and vernacular reports of the Stevens compact and the Treaty of Olympia range widely in content and detail. Interpreters, as the scholar Alexandra Harmon (2008, 17) has cogently surmised, cannot hope to understand treaties (or the lack of treaties) without considering the complexity and variability of the power relations under which treaties were and continue to be interpreted and played out. The story of the failed treaty is an important one for the Cowlitz and is examined elsewhere in this book (chapter 4). Because they never treated with the United States government, the Cowlitz often were at a disadvantage in the changing political and cultural landscape that was Washington Territory and became Washington State.

1855 AND AFTER: THE TRIALS

On January 25, 1856, the U.S. government entered into the Treaty of Olympia with the Quinault and Quileute Tribes of Washington State. The Chinook, the Chehalis, the Cowlitz, and other tribal constituents present at the Chehalis River Treaty were not signatories. The initial reservation granted by this treaty for the Quinault and Quileute Indians was ten thousand acres. The Treaty of Olympia was significant for the Cowlitz in that it allowed for other tribes to be consolidated upon the reservation, tribes whose land actually lay elsewhere. In 1871, a decade and a half later, the Indian Appropriations Act was passed by Congress and President Ulysses Grant, prohibiting federal officials to treat with Indian tribes. Lawyer Steven Pevar (1997, 7), in *The Rights of Indians and Tribes*, has written that "Congress no longer considered Indian tribes as independent nations. From then on, Congress dealt with Indians by passing laws, which, unlike treaties, do not require tribal consent. If Congress wanted to take a tribe's land, all it had to do was pass a law to that effect." This reality obviously had disastrous effects for the Cowlitz as well as for every other tribe living within the United States.

On November 4, 1873, President Grant expanded the Quinault Reservation by roughly two hundred thousand acres, allowing for the Quinault and Quileute and "other tribes of fish-eating Indians on the Pacific coast" (the Cowlitz among them) to live upon it. Grant created a larger reservation at Quinault in hopes of consolidating any outlying tribes in the area into one isolated unit of land, hence freeing up millions of acres for white settlers who were quickly populating Washington Territory following the Donation Land Claim Act of 1850. The Donation Land Claim Act specified that claim titles awarded to settlers would not be given until treaties with tribes were secured, treaties in which tribes in the area explicitly gave up their land. The two hundred thousand expanded acres Grant offered tribal peoples were thickly forested and largely uninhabitable, especially for those Natives accustomed to living on a prairie.

Around 1868, when a decree of sovereign immunity by the federal government ruled that the Cowlitz and other Indians could not sue them for loss and damages, the Cowlitz began to interact regularly with the federal government through engagement with various agencies. Although the Dawes Act of 1887, also known as the General Allotment Act, proved both a blessing and a curse for the Cowlitz, it was patently disastrous for many tribes. The act was designed to break up their lands and system of government by creating individual parcels of land and by allowing white settlers to live in reservation territory. An excerpt from the *National Congress of American Indians Handbook* (1999, 9) reads that in the years "1887 to 1934, the U. S. Government took over 90 million acres of Native lands, nearly two-thirds of reservation lands, from the tribes without compensation and gave it to settlers." In addition, the U.S. government's policy was aggressive in its effort to assimilate Native people. Indian children were sent to boarding schools; Natives were forbidden their sacred ceremonies and access to their languages; and the effort of religious missionaries to convert Natives was fierce. Because of such deleterious governmental policies, the Cowlitz were devastated in the century after European contact, but they managed to survive. Though their culture and language diminished and they intermarried with settlers and took on nontraditional occupations, they managed to maintain their identity as a people. Many Cowlitz learned to work within the system as well: they learned to organize according to the federal government's standard, and they started the process for both land claims and federal recognition from the late 1800s on.

ALLOTMENT AND LAND GRANTS

On March 4, 1911, Congress passed the Quinault Allotment Act, allowing other tribes affiliated with the Treaty of Olympia to secure allotments on the Quinault Reservation. A number of Cowlitz people filed for allotments at this time and fought with other tribes to secure them throughout the 1900s. Their efforts, along with those of the Chehalis, Chinook, and other small tribes of western Washington, resulted in the 1931 Supreme Court decision *Halbert v. United States*, which ruled that the Cowlitz and other tribal peoples could have allotments on the expanded Quinault Reservation. Subsequently, between 1932 and 1934, the Cowlitz took approximately sixty allotments at Quinault.

Two decades before the receipt of these allotments, at the turn of the nineteenth century, the Cowlitz had begun an effort to secure a jurisdictional act by which they could file in the U.S. Court of Claims for an opportunity to sue for the value of the lands taken from them in southwestern Washington, the site of their aboriginal territory. The Cowlitz began to remediate for the loss of their aboriginal land. This resulted in a series of some dozen or so bills introduced to and ultimately failing in Congress. This was a dark time for the Cowlitz, and they foundered until the creation of the Indian Claims Commission in 1946. The Claims Commission gave tribal peoples a method by which they could approach Congress and present claims against the United States. The Cowlitz people still had meetings, the people still gathered, but the mood among them was one of discouragement.

Beckham, who has worked for the Cowlitz as a hired historian, notes that although they were "without a ratified treaty and not removed from their homelands, the Cowlitz were under a series of Bureau of Indian Affairs (BIA) jurisdictions for decades" and were included in western agency reports on the Coast and throughout the Puget Sound from as early as 1856 to as late as 1957 (Beckham 1991, 2). The BIA had many other administrative exchanges with the Cowlitz as well, ranging from inclusion in annual reports and supervision of sales in Cowlitz land and assets, to enrollment in BIA schools and issuance of state fishing and Indian hunting licenses (called "blue cards"). These myriad dealings with the government did much to secure the Cowlitz's identity. Throughout this time the Cowlitz kept a close relationship with the BIA, with continued contact with federal, state, and local governments. Despite their active involvement, however, it seemed the Cowlitz were at risk, for in 1953 termination was declared the long-range goal of federal Indian policy, with the bulk of tribes marked for termination located in California and Oregon.

The fear of, and effect of, termination on tribes was severe. A terminated tribe would be "ordered to distribute its land and property to its members and to dissolve its government. The tribe could no longer exercise any governmental powers, and all of its property was taken away. The tribe was essentially being forced into political extinction" (Pevar 1997, 10). Termination meant that the trust that existed between the federal government and the tribes would effectively be ended; government-made promises to tribes in exchange for their land and pacifism would be broken; services rendered to tribes would be cut. In 1953 a congressional bill that would have terminated federal relations with the landless tribes of western Washington who had not entered into treaties failed to pass in Congress. Despite this failure, however, the BIA took matters in its own hands, claiming administrative authority as if the bill had passed and essentially dropped the Cowlitz off its roster, treating the tribe as if it had been terminated; the BIA managed the tribe's fiscal affairs during this time. Throughout this contentious period, the Cowlitz hired an anthropologist, Verne Ray, who started his research on area tribes in the 1930s and conducted additional research for the Cowlitz in 1965 and 1966 in an effort to help secure their land claim. Ray's research (1938 and 1966) contributed to the success of Docket 218, the Cowlitz land claims settlement, and was later used in the Cowlitz's initial petition for tribal recognition, submitted in the 1970s.

THE COWLITZ LAND CLAIMS

As part of a plan to end governmental intervention into tribal affairs, Congress passed the Indian Claims Commission Act on August 13, 1946. This established a special tribunal in which Native peoples could bring land claims cases against the U.S. government and was intended as a means to end Native claims to land in the United States once and for all. A commission was formed that might adjudicate complaints of Indian tribes, bands, and other identifiable groups of American Indians who might be able to receive land, money, and other compensation for losses suffered since the time of white occupation. For the first time, Indian oral testimony was accepted as proof of land use and occupancy.

By the time of its dissolution in 1978, the Indian Claims Commission (ICC) had heard more than five hundred claims. Anthropologist Pamela Wallace (2002, 748) has noted that during this time "the term tribe became an issue for definition and clarification, wherein the government established certain criteria for determining which groups would qualify for claim submission. In an attempt to include those groups that might not be recognized as a tribe or band, the commission designed the phrase 'identifiable group' to facilitate the task of bringing to finality all Indian claims." The ICC did not anticipate any glitches or inherent problems in processing the land claims, and while Congress originally gave the ICC a decade-long tenure, it continued to hear claims for thirty-two years. Historians, anthropologists, and genealogists would be summoned in force to create the thousands upon thousands of documents that served as evidence for claims.

With the formation of the ICC, the Cowlitz saw that they might yet have a chance to claim compensation for their lost land and so submitted a petition in 1951. In 1965 the result of the formal petition, called Docket 218, was an agreement by the government to award the Cowlitz money for some of their lost lands, a $1.5 million settlement based on the 1863 federal taking date. This seemingly arbitrary taking date was established because the Court of Claims—which existed as of 1855—had allowed American citizens to file against the government. Its rules were changed on March 3, 1863, so that tribes could not sue the government on treaty issues without express permission of the government to waive sovereignty and allow litigation. In 1969 the ICC granted a favorable decision on the Cowlitz land claim, maintaining that the United States had "'exercised such domination and control' over Cowlitz Indian Tribal lands that the tribe had been deprived of its aboriginal title without its consent" (R. Torner 1994, 25). However, no settlement was made and so by "an act of July 1, 1973, Congress [would] appropriate monies to pay a judgment awarded in favor to the Cowlitz Tribe of Indians of the State of Washington by the ICC in Docket 218. The monies [were] in compensation for the taking of the United States over 100 years ago of Cowlitz Tribal lands [sic] located in what is now Lewis, Cowlitz, Clark, Pierce, Skamania and Wahkiakum counties in the state" (ibid., 25).

In 1973 the Cowlitz Tribe was summoned to a special meeting with federal officials. The meeting was contentious, as the initial offer for compensation is popularly believed to have been some sixty-five cents an acre, a price set at 1863 land prices. Beckham's research on this issue yields further information. He writes that "the [ICC] focused on the value of the land at the 'date of taking,'" and the research conducted by those who assessed both the "date of taking" and the "value of the land" was insufficient and hurt tribal interests (Beckham 2005, 9). Although experts assessing the value of the land taken from tribes considered many things, at no time did they "take into account that in many parts of the United States the value of the land had [already] been established by Congress," and furthermore that by the "General Land Act of 1800 . . . Congress had fixed minimum values for lands" in the Pacific Northwest (ibid., 10). This value was $1.25 per acre, set for anyone "seeking to purchase [land] at the General Land Office" (ibid., 10). According to Beckham (ibid.), in "none of the cases it considered from the Pacific Northwest did the Indian Claims Commission determine that Indian land [was] taken subsequent to 1855." From this already small amount, deductions were taken from the estimated award for services tribes had received from the federal government, before their claim (ibid.). Through a deeply flawed assessment, the ICC underestimated Cowlitz boundaries for their "Usual and Accustomed Territory," ignoring "watersheds and logical land use by the Cowlitz. The Commission awarded the Cowlitz approximately $0.50 per acre at a value set in 1863. It ignored the statute of 1850 that fixed the minimum value of lands in the Pacific Northwest at $1.25 per acre to any purchaser" (ibid., 19).

For some Cowlitz people the fact that they won a land settlement with the government was compensation enough. For others, however, the awarded price per acre was a stinging slap in the face. The government was not offering money for mere acreage, after all. The money offered (ultimately to be about ninety-three cents an acre) was truly incommensurate pay for rich southwestern Washington land bordering U.S. Interstate 5 and near major cities and the Pacific Ocean. No offer could compensate for the lives, the land, and the profound loss suffered by each member of the Cowlitz Indian Tribe. Some Cowlitz knew this, and expected more. Others felt, fearing government reprisal or no award at all, that they needed to accept the offer, cut their losses, and move on.

Clifford Wilson served as Cowlitz chair through much of this time, from 1961 until his sudden death in 1972. He was succeeded by Roy Wilson (no relation), who headed the Cowlitz Indian Tribe for a decade, from 1972 to 1982. Roy Wilson inherited the stormy conflict and complicated issues resulting from the Docket 218 settlement. Cowlitz chairman John Barnett has noted the long and demonstrable history of conflict and resolution, factions and fellowship, in the Cowlitz Tribe. In his memory the tribe was always able to surmount its differences and pull together to make decisions and act as a unified group. In 1973, however, the Cowlitz Tribe was unable to do so. The tribal disagreements and splintering resulting from the dissent over the proposed land claims award resulted in another profound disappointment for the Cowlitz people. Arguing that there was factionalism in the tribe, the Bureau of Indian Affairs held the Cowlitz Docket 218 settlement money.

According to Cowlitz sources, the tribe was told that until they secured federal recognition, they would not get their Docket 218 funds. It would take another two decades for a compromise to be reached and for Docket 218 to be partially disbursed in late fall 2004. At this point the Cowlitz could simply have quit their struggle. They had spent nearly a century embroiled with the federal government in an effort to reclaim what they felt was rightly theirs. Instead, the tribe once again summoned its resources. They began the federal acknowledgment process, which would take an additional twenty-six years and countless resources.

BACK TO THE DRAWING BOARD: FEDERAL ACKNOWLEDGMENT

Federal recognition, also called acknowledgment, once meant cognitive recognition of a tribe by the U.S. government. Simply put, federal officials noticed that a tribe existed, according to their biases of what constituted a legitimate tribal entity. Today the term "tribe" is often used to describe the genealogical descendents of such a tribal entity. A "recognized" Indian tribe is one that has political status under the U.S. Constitution and is afforded the benefits of that status. These benefits are not to be underestimated. The importance of federal recognition for tribal continuity and sustenance, however problematic, cannot be overemphasized.

By the 1870s federal recognition of tribes had dropped precipitously. The diminishing threat of tribal warfare and an executive order calling for cessation of treaty-making contributed to the decrease in tribal recognition. Some sixty years later, the tenor of federal and tribal relationships changed again with the institution of the Indian Reorganization Act (IRA) in the 1930s. The act's main provisions were to restore Native land and preserve Native resources, to create opportunities for economic development in Indian country, and to bolster tribal self-governance. Federal policies toward Natives changed in the Department of the Interior, influenced by Commissioner of Indian Affairs John Collier, whose strong advocacy sought to protect tribal interests. Tribal recognition concerns rose again with the passage of the IRA, which called for the recognition of a tribe based on its existence as a specific legal entity, a very different criterion from the earlier standard of mere cognitive recognition.

Lawyer Felix S. Cohen wrote the widely respected *Handbook of Federal Indian Law* in 1942. The Cohen criteria were used to determine the eligibility of tribes to organize according to Section 16 of the Indian Reorganization Act. His criteria settled around a tribe's relationship with the federal government that could be traced historically by documentation and by ethnographic interview, thus relying upon sociohistorical (such as treaty relations, legislation, and whether or not the tribe was recognized as such by other tribes) as well as genealogical factors. Tribal councils, as evidence of unity and organization, counted as one of these deciding factors, as did other political entities the tribe might have in place that could exercise authority over its members. From the mid-1930s until 1978, the U.S. government determined tribal existence based on whether or not a tribe (a) "had treaty relations with the U.S.; (b) had been denominated a tribe by act of Congress or executive order; (c) had been treated as having collective rights in tribal lands or funds; (d) had been treated by a tribe or band by other tribes; or (e) had exercised political authority over its members through a tribal council or other governmental forms" (NARF 2000, 2).

In 1978, at the close of the Indian Claims Commission, the Bureau of Indian Affairs and its subsidiary, the Branch of Acknowledgment and Research, took over the federal recognition process. With its takeover of the process, the Bureau of Indian Affairs Branch of Acknowledgment and Research (BIA BAR), originally called the Federal Acknowledgement Project, instigated criteria for recognition tempered by Cohen's criteria but was likewise mired in the romance of the Indian Reorganization Act. Scholar Roy Cook has noted that the BIA BAR regulations were significant. They did not and do not refer to treaties or other federal acts as a means of locating "prior federal recognition" of tribes (R. Cook 2003, 2). He writes: "Petitioning for federal recognition is an exhaustive process that includes submitting a letter of intent requesting acknowledgment; submitting a petition with supporting documents; undergoing a preliminary review of the petition for the purpose of technical assistance; awaiting notice of active consideration; being actively involved in the BAR staff's consideration of the petition; awaiting the proposed finding on federal recognition being published in the Federal Register; undergoing public comment; and awaiting the final determination of federal recognition" (ibid., 2).

Scholar Samuel Cook (2002, 92) has indicted the federal acknowledgment process and criteria, claiming they "reflect essentialist and contradictory notions based on reified images of what constitutes an 'Indian' and a 'tribe,' and ignore the fluid character of tribal identities and social configurations." The Bureau of Indian Affairs has been roundly and repeatedly criticized for having "no systematic method of applying the criteria to determine which tribes were eligible for its services," and the BIA BAR, according to law professor Rachael Paschal (1991, 218), has relied on a "mixture of court opinions, limited statutory guidance, treaty law, and evolving departmental policy and practices to determine tribal status." Roy Cook and others have noted the arduous process to which tribes must submit in their effort to secure federal recognition. It is a process necessitating a team of BIA BAR experts, among them an anthropologist, who review each petition. If a tribe fails in its efforts, "the only opportunities to contest the adverse findings is to request reconsideration from the Assistant Secretary through the Secretary of Interior, or seek an appeal through the Interior Board of Indian Appeals, or ultimately through federal court review" (R. Cook 2003, 2). The burden of proof thus rests with the tribe, and it is an incredible burden—indeed, one that many tribes cannot bear.

As of February 6, 2001, of the 250 tribal groups who had either filed a letter of interest or petitioned for acknowledgment since 1978, only 15 had been recognized by the Department of the Interior, roughly 7 percent. The process is slow and incredibly painstaking. The process is costly and the burden of proof rests with the petitioning tribe. In September 1975, when the Cowlitz lined up with other tribes seeking federal recognition through the anticipated new process (to appear in 1978), they were sixteenth in the queue. Although the Federal Acknowledgment Process was not formalized until 1978, the Cowlitz petition was at the ready three years earlier, in September 1975. That petition was transferred from the Bureau of Indian Affairs to the Federal Acknowledgment Project in 1978, with the creation of that office. Twenty-seven years later, in January 2002, they were awarded federal recognition. Twenty-nine years later, in 2004, their land claims (Docket 218) were finally partially released.

The Cowlitz history of engagement with the federal government suggests incredible tenacity and unwavering vision for their goals. In ongoing efforts to secure their land, the Cowlitz had to anchor their identity repeatedly in community settings. Tribal chair John Barnett and spiritual leader Roy Wilson—men who are characteristic of the Cowlitz and yet rare in their depth of time and service to the tribe—tell the Cowlitz story as often and in as many ways as they can. They select stories that reflect their priorities for the tribe, and they relay Cowlitz history during General Council time, when Cowlitz people gather by the hundreds to hear tribal news. What they talk about is Cowlitz history, a history they believe belongs to them personally and hence to the Cowlitz people; it is not a mere academic exercise in paternalistic protectionism.

Barnett and Wilson have committed to memory Cowlitz history, which they tell again and again, through landscape and legend, myth and personal history. It is a history they have lived, which they will not let fade into obscurity. It is a history they inhabit, when they take the space and time of Cowlitz General Council meetings. Psychologist Michael Roe, who has worked with the Cowlitz since the early 1980s, has cited the Cowlitz as a rare group that has managed to sustain its native identity, despite their having never treated with or received tribal land from the government. "Ethnic groups in conflict are rarely interested in giving up their cultural identities and histories," Roe (2003, 56) has written; it is a rare people indeed, he declares, who are able to stay together despite the forces of history.

SOCIAL MEMORY: A CONSIDERATION

How exactly does a tribe stay together, especially when under pressure? How do they see themselves as a tribe when that very definition is being questioned and scrutinized? In his article on Cowlitz survival and identity-making, Roe (ibid., 66) asserts that as "members of groups share social memories, these become context and content for what will be jointly recalled and commemorated in the future ... with social forgetting constructed the same [way] as social remembering." Roe adheres to a model of memory construction which demonstrates that groups often construct and reinforce positive memories to show their "continuity, collective self-esteem, distinctiveness, efficacy and cohesion," and he considers the means by which the Cowlitz Tribe constructs identity and social memories (ibid., 66). Roe claims that social remembering and the "notion of continuity is demonstrated when members explain their present identity with consistent constructions of the past; for example, the Cowlitz people consistently assert their 'Indianness' in relationship to their aboriginal ancestors" (ibid., 66). Ethnic identity and social memory therefore "have provided [community] stability and empowerment for the Cowlitz Indians [and] it has been precisely that continuity in their identity and memories which has perpetuated conflict with the U. S. government—a government that has intended that the Cowlitz simply assimilate into U.S. society and no longer raise challenges to it" (ibid., 56).

Cowlitz history is a history replete with conflict. It is a history of acculturation, but not of assimilation. Roe (ibid., 57) explains that "acculturation refers to the process of culture change, which results from direct and continuous contact between two or more cultural groups." While acculturation influences are mutual, most changes occur in the less dominant group. There are conceptual problems with the most common acculturation model, Roe notes. In this model, less dominant groups are always seen as assimilated into the dominant group, and it is merely a matter of degree and time until the less dominant group evaporates without a trace. The Cowlitz Tribe, however, represents a group that has retained its history and remembered its past. At the heart of this book is my exploration of how this retention has occurred. Roe notes that "since the day in 1855 when the Cowlitz refused to sign a treaty with the U.S. government, they have vigorously confronted federal, state and local governments, even inviting arrest as they exercised rights denied to them" (ibid., 56). The Cowlitz people, specifically the tribe's leaders but also individual members, have constructed their past in cooperation with and in resistance to these "vigorous" confrontations with the government at all levels. Individual efforts to sustain Cowlitz culture through performance of narrative and its genres occur and create particular stories for the tribe. These performances influence the group and its collective means of remembering.

THE FRAGILITY OF GROUP IDENTITY

It is a cool, wet Monday in December at the Cowlitz Longview administrative office. Cowlitz people are milling to the clinic for services and therapies, the Christmas tree hangs heavily with baroque ornaments, most of them miniatures of southwestern Indian regalia, the phone rings off the hook, and harried Cowlitz employees with numerous job titles run in and out of the office. Others, less well known, enter the office hopefully with enrollment papers in hand. In the back rooms the Cultural Committee is gathered, smudging participants with sage. Next door, Natural Resources is meeting with the Washington State Department of Fish and Wildlife regarding an endangered bat. The accountant is down from Saint Mary's administrative office located in Toledo, Washington, and he lectures impatiently on the protocol for completing purchase orders. Winter birds are chirping outside, the heater is broken in area C, and the receptionist is cozied up with her mom practicing the upper Cowlitz language and taking notes, making personal taxonomies. The librarian runs in with the mail and gives flowers to her auntie, who is head administrator. It is a typical day at the tribal office. The number of employees has grown from a dozen or so to nearly forty this year. Most employees are relatives, living within miles of each other, despite the fact that the tribe has no reservation lands as yet. Tonight they will share dinner and a TV program, go to bed, get up tomorrow and do it again. Most Cowlitz tribal activities center on General Council, held twice a year, or the two sites of administration in Toledo and Longview, Washington, where programs are gaining steam and people gather for different events and services.

In Dorothy Noyes's important essay "Group" (1996), she distinguishes between the measurable, daily interactions of a group, called the "network," and the more elusive and qualitative "felt reality" that is perpetually constructed and reconstructed within groups. "Felt reality" occurs in the community's social imagination, which is part of the network of daily contacts. When grappling with definitions of group, Noyes is careful to distinguish between the "locus of culture" and the "focus of identity." First, there is the network, which exists as an empirical network of relations. Next, there is the "social imaginary in which performance occurs," which participants experience as their felt reality. Says Noyes (1996, 451), "the word group is shorthand for the interaction between the two." In matters of historical or other performances among groups, she writes, "performance that constructs the community ideologically and emotionally also strengthens or changes the shape of networks by promoting interaction; it may even have the effect of breaking up a network by redrawing the boundaries within it" (ibid., 471).

Noyes considers the importance of the multiplex relationship. Unlike a single strand relationship, a multiplex relationship is built on numerous factors, such as "working together [where] the multiplex relationship is one in which my sister-in-law works with me, lives in the house down the block, and spends her free time in my kitchen, chatting" (ibid., 457). The multiplex is a structure but contains relational elements such as the emotional content and intensity of a relationship, how long it has lasted, and how frequently it is engaged. Within the network multiplex is the "dense multiplex." The dense multiplex, Noyes explains, is also likely to be the repository of conservative vernacular culture. Characterized by frequent interactions, a high degree of solidarity, and an equally high degree of social control, this sort of network has sufficient integrity to resist the pressure of hegemonic norms. Many Cowlitz people fit Noyes's definition of the dense multiplex, as seen in the Cowlitz Longview administrative office. These Cowlitz are relatives. They often work together, and if they do not, they see each other a minimum of once a month to daily; most Cowlitz people do activities outside of work and attend tribal meetings together. They often live near each other. Most important, they see their relationships as enduring, literally lasting a lifetime. During the most heated of disputes, people will sigh and say, "but we're family," as a means of dismissing any claim to enduring rift or anger. The duration of Cowlitz relationships is usually long term, seen as bounded in genealogy, in history, and in family emotional ties. The Cowlitz place a high priority on staying together, no matter what, which reinforces the themes of persistence, endurance, and familial belonging that run through individual Cowlitz narratives.

But these relationships are in perpetual danger of falling away. Historical forces have seen Cowlitz scatter, despite community ties, not merely to other parts of Washington State but to all over the United States. To survive, these Cowlitz people had to adapt to the dominant society. This adaptation changed their lifeways significantly, especially since the Cowlitz are a landless tribe with no treaty, having to take whatever measures necessary to survive both as individuals and as a tribe. Cowlitz chairman John Barnett (1989, 4) articulated this well in an interview:

> I think this is one of the big problems that the Cowlitz people have had: by staying in their aboriginal lands and, in many cases, intermarrying with whites, they are probably one generation ahead of Indians on reservations today. But this does not mean they are not Indians. I think that the very fact that the Cowlitz are one half to a generation ahead of other tribes has caused them more problems than anything else. I think the federal government twenty years from now [will] see [other tribal peoples] as no different from the Cowlitz today. We are one generation ahead, and it is due to the fact that we were forced to assimilate with the white people and through intermarriages. Looks has [sic] nothing to do with our Indianness.

Barnett insists that simply because the Indian integrates, it does not mean that he is assimilated. Like models of assimilation that allow for many dimensions and variations, I contend that the Cowlitz leaders, and by extension many Cowlitz people, are dynamic, as is their identity. This dynamism and survival can be demonstrated and explained—at least in part—by paying close attention to the particular genres of typical Cowlitz performance.

Epigraph: Wilkinson 2005, 16.

CHAPTER 3

Historical Discourse and the Use of Landscape

Genres of Attachment

CHAPTER 2 DETAILED THE HISTORY AS WELL AS THE CURRENT situation of the Cowlitz, of the realities that threatened their identity as a tribe and as individual tribal members. This chapter examines the process of meaning-making in performance. Performance is one of the key ways a tribe (especially a landless one) creates and maintains a shared group identity. Let us consider a very important Cowlitz General Council meeting and Chairman John Barnett's evocation of the legendary Mount Saint Helens. The Cowlitz's attachment to their land is a common theme, existing not only in the literature and ethnography about the Cowlitz but also in many of my interviews with Cowlitz members. Other significant and recurring narratives among the Cowlitz I interviewed will also be addressed in this chapter.

A sense of the importance of land to the Cowlitz consistently arose in these narratives. Ecology can reveal an evolution of a language and lifeways; it can demonstrate the long-standing priorities and values of a people and an understanding of a people's place on the land and their long-term relationship with it. When ecology is coupled with the idea of performance, it allows us to discuss instances in which Cowlitz connection to the land can be examined in terms of its narrative priorities. When considering my interviews with Cowlitz people and leaders, I wondered who among them maintained their sense of identity and attachment against the forces of externally imposed categories of culture. I wondered what sort of identity

Cowlitz individuals were able to maintain. How do these individuals translate to the group their priorities for an identity?

I begin with the specific use of a Cowlitz place-name, Mount Saint Helens, used by Chairman John Barnett at the Cowlitz General Council on November 6, 2004—the day of the announcement of the release of Cowlitz Indian Claims Commission (ICC) Docket 218, the long-awaited settlement between the Cowlitz and the federal government about proper compensation for lost land. Barnett's use of the place-name, his evocation of the place for his listeners, demonstrates the reciprocal relationship that exists between the narrative event (discussion of Cowlitz grief and anger), the narrated item (Mount Saint Helens), and the context in which it is summoned (at Cowlitz General Council). A close look at the genres emerging in Barnett's narrative gives us insight into the nature of the relationship created at the moment of a narrator's skilled summoning of a mountain and a metaphor. In the context of Cowlitz General Council, and embedded in the historical context of the release of Docket 218, Barnett discusses some general facts about Mount Saint Helens and its eruption in 1980.

While at first this simple mention of Mount Saint Helens may seem to have little to do with past times before European contact, which are usually seen in a positive light, we will come to see that the mention does in fact have much to do with what has come before. Through a consideration of place-names and a discussion of the symbolic content of landscape, we see that for the Cowlitz leader and those who listen to him, the mere mention of Mount Saint Helens evokes an overwhelmingly positive historical and symbolic connection of the Cowlitz to their ancestral land. While the beneficent past is not mentioned, the history resting on shared anger and grief is evoked symbolically in Mount Saint Helens, a dazzlingly eruptive fact of Cowlitz prairie life. The mountain looms large in non-Native popular imagination since its last major explosion in 1980 as a surprisingly destructive force, something to be avoided at all costs. But the Cowlitz tend to understand the place much differently.

By favorable comparison of a mountain to a people (and reference to their shared and potentially explosive anger), Barnett simply but powerfully demonstrates an understanding of the people's shared identity and attachment to the land of the Cowlitz Prairie, from whose vantage Mount

Saint Helens can be seen most clearly. Anthropologist Charles Briggs (1988, 59), in his book *Competence in Performance: The Creativity of Tradition in Mexicano Verbal Art*, has called this form of narrative construction "historical discourse." He claims that it contains four different basic types of narrative that one can observe in the course of elder interactions. These four types are "competitive displays of oral historical knowledge and rhetorical skill between small groups of elders; allusions to bygone days in conversations between persons between thirty and sixty years of age; noncompetitive discussions between elders; and pedagogically oriented exchanges between elders and their juniors" (ibid., 59).

Briggs's third category of "noncompetitive discussions among elders" sheds light on what Barnett does in his discussion of the mountain. Briggs describes this category as clearly performative but highly dialogic. By this he means the discourses rise from a "cooperation" of elders to develop a "vision of the past." While Barnett acts with great independence, he also relies on his long-standing relationships with other tribal council members—some of whom have sat with him on the council for decades—to create the basic principles and serve as an assenting (or at least witnessing) group for his discussions, especially as they occur during General Council. It is there that, in succession, different council members representing commissions and committees share both floor and microphone to make announcements and update members about administrative and other activities.

Briggs's fourth category of "pedagogical discourse," when elders speak specifically to guide the younger generation's understanding of the past, is important here too. Pedagogical discourse displays in its performance how circumstances have changed for a people and how the meaning of that change emerges in the present. I estimate that at any given General Council meeting about a third of the Cowlitz present are under the age of forty. Pedagogical discourse naturally has utility in a meeting where children and their parents gather, as one of its chief functions is to teach values and persuade the young to adopt proper behavior.

It is also productive to look at Barnett's narrative in light of Briggs's discussion of the historical discourse among the elders of Cordova. The Cordovan are a group of elders in northern New Mexico. Cordova was settled by Spaniards in the early eighteenth century and the area remains linguistically and culturally distinct. The Cordovan elders carry responsibility for keeping Cordovan stories and culture alive for the youth and their methods of doing so parallel the Cowlitz elders' ways of keeping culture. There is an interesting parallel to be drawn between these two groups, as the Cordovan elders, like Barnett, shoulder the responsibility for "ensuring the vitality of Mexicano culture and the survival of its bearers through *la plática de los viejitos de antes*. This task is fulfilled through performances by elders in the company of both their peers and of their juniors. This 'talk' is seen as embodying the collective identity of the community and of Mexicano society in general and failure to transmit this talk to succeeding generations means that outside values—we could say outside definitions—will supplant and destroy Cordovan Society" (Briggs 1988, 94). Thus it is with the Cowlitz.

SITES OF HISTORICAL DISCOURSE FOR THE COWLITZ

As an important elder and longtime chairman of the Cowlitz Tribe, John Barnett uses the privilege of his office to reinforce the values held in common for the Cowlitz. He provides the people with vital recitations of their history, especially that of their struggle against the federal government. These recitations help to create group solidarity and a much-needed sense of historical and tribal continuity. Through artistic use of spoken language and artistic verbal performance, observes the folklorist Richard Bauman (1972, 32), "language usage . . . takes on special significance above and beyond its referential information dimension through the systematic elaboration of any component of verbal behavior in such a way that this component calls attention to itself and is perceived as uncommon or special in a particular context." Bauman's term for performance, "frame," is useful to consider here as it denotes a situation in which "basic referential" language is transformed, signaling the listener, or "auditor," to comprehend that although the language used may seem literal and ordinary, the listener should understand what is being said in a "special sense." This leads them to see that performance "sets up, or represents, an interpretive frame" marking the manner in which the "messages being communicated are to be understood" (Bauman 1977, 9).

These frames usually occur in specifically designated places. For John Barnett, one such space is the Saint Mary's Mission, where General Council meetings are held. Saint Mary's is a historical site, near to what once was a Hudson's Bay subsidiary farm on the Cowlitz Prairie, standing on Cowlitz aboriginal ground. The Cowlitz refer to the whole of the property—its church and cemetery as well as the old school in which they gather—as "Saint Mary's," although the cemetery and church are alternately and more formally known by the name of Saint Francis Xavier. Saint Mary's, as I call it in keeping with Cowlitz custom, was recently reacquired as tribal property. Before that, General Council meetings were held at the Cowlitz Prairie Grange Hall, a communal space located a couple of miles from the mission. Saint Mary's Mission, when a Hudson's Bay site, was the place where Catholic priests Francois Norbert Blanchet and Modeste Demers landed in the 1830s to minister to fur company employees and convert the Indians to Catholicism. It still houses a convent and small church as well as a cemetery where many Cowlitz families are buried. In an ironic turn of events, the nuns of Saint Mary's sold some of the grounds back to Cowlitz Tribal Housing in 2002. Most Cowlitz are aware of the deep history of Saint Mary's. Many went to school there as children. It stands on majestic prairie land, near the Cowlitz River and in the shadow of Mounts St. Helens, Adams, and Rainier.

The anthropologist Darleen Fitzpatrick (quoted in J. Irwin 1994, 50) has written that since 1915, the Cowlitz meetings are the tribe's centering event and that "meetings in the aboriginal territory provide kin connectedness, information about Cowlitz cultural and historical identity and define their relationships with the larger society and federal government." Cowlitz General Council is held in a high school–size gymnasium. The floors are worn and wooden, and at the southern end of the gym stands a basketball hoop slightly the worse for wear. The northern side of the space, where twenty-two Tribal Council members sit facing outward toward the larger audience, is bracketed by a theater stage, complete with thick curtain and, behind and below, what might once have been a green room but now is filled with sports equipment. The overall effect of the arrangement can be likened to a state senate floor. The building itself is beautiful but rather old and, like many a building in soggy southwestern Washington, it feels slightly damp and smells slightly musty. Halls bound the General Council room to the west, and across the way is the children's room, where Cowlitz kids spend the day, playing and hanging out with each other. Their sounds are buffered from the General Council proper, but children are usually invited in to sing and play drums or be part of honors ceremonies.

The front quarter of the room is bounded by tribal council members, who sit facing west, looking at the tribal membership. The arrangement denotes a clear line of authority, and the membership rarely steps forward across the space between leaders and audience to talk to council members, certainly never during the meeting proper. This line is only broken when the chair invites members to take their turn at the microphone. At breaks, council members step out to greet their relatives. Even this gesture, in the temporal and physical confines of Cowlitz General Council, is unusual. Tacit rules of deportment and display of authority are clear, if unspoken, and reinforced by the arrangement of chairs and tables. During lunch breaks, as members move into the hallway and out toward the kitchen and cafeteria, these lines become indistinct: the chairman sits anywhere, and council members spread out or move into the kitchen to help serve and clean up. During the meal, which is always served during a General Council meeting, the elders are served first and sit first. It is in very bad form to cut in front of, or eat before, an elder. To do so demonstrates misapprehension of an important group rule.

This setup of General Council has deviated little in the fifteen years I have attended (since the mid-1990s), although the technology used has grown more sophisticated. In front of the council members stands a single microphone and stand, and beside it—as often as not—someone to help with technical issues. PowerPoint and other computer-generated presentations have become standard. The microphone is an interesting object of importance in the room. It stands as a clear and solitary divider between council and members. Its use is controlled by the chairman, who regulates the microphone and serves as the emcee for the day's events. He controls the flow. This command of the microphone is especially important when the audience is invited up to give their opinion on an issue. The invitation to queue up to speak marks an important cite of regulation. Often speakers will address a topic with passion or anger. But though they may speak long, and sometimes harshly, this event is tightly scripted and tightly controlled, to be discontinued any time Chairman Barnett feels enough information has been heard.

Members of General Council can take the microphone only under two circumstances: if an item is up for vote, and there has to be discussion, or at the end of the meeting, for the good of the order. Meetings can run long, and if a particular issue to vote on or motion is on the floor, things can get contentious and go long. Chairman Barnett controls this flow, and he tends to be very liberal about letting people speak their minds. The General Council is similar to any town meeting in its passions, effusions, and conflicts. Indeed, General Council reads like a town meeting, but one in which all the townspeople are—to greater or lesser degree—related. The interests of the group are heterogeneous, but the group gathers in common as the Cowlitz Indian Tribe. Since the Cowlitz has no reservation land, the General Council meeting provides them the welcome opportunity to gather as a group. This is the venue in which John Barnett rises to give his chairman's speech, his semiannual performance for the Cowlitz group.

NOVEMBER 6, 2004:
FALL GENERAL COUNCIL

It is 10 A.M. and a sunny Saturday in November on the Cowlitz Prairie near Toledo, Washington. The large gym of Saint Mary's Mission, cold an hour ago, is quickly warming with the mass of people filing in, buzzing around and greeting each other in excitement. The walls echo with chatter. On this late fall day, the fruit trees are laden with Gravenstein apples and the mountains surrounding the area are in clear view. It is a perfect, pellucid day in which the Cowlitz people have gathered for their semiannual General Council meeting.

The Cowlitz meeting of November 6, 2004, is ready to begin and the meeting is called to order. The gavel lands soundly, and the racket of the crowd begins to quiet. Holding the gavel comfortably in his right hand is John Barnett, chairman of the Cowlitz General Council. He is no stranger to the front of the room; he has held office for decades and has been the chairman of the General Council since 1981. Nevertheless, today is a standout day, even in the many years that Barnett has led the Cowlitz Tribe. It's an important day: Barnett will announce the Cowlitz land settlement, known as Docket 218, and its long-in-coming disbursal. The tribal council officers answer "present" at roll call, last council's minutes are approved, and guests are welcomed and introduced. Following the treasurer's report, Chairman Barnett approached the gathering to give his formal report. The chairman's report is a vital part of the Cowlitz General Council meeting, and Barnett covers some important issues. He clears his throat and waits expectantly, watching the crowd. He grips the microphone in his large hand, and it buzzes a bit with feedback as the room stills to listen.

The contemporary Cowlitz tribal government is comprised of a General Council of all its members and an elected tribal council of twenty-two, three of whom act as chair, vice chair, and secretary to General Council and are represented at tribal council monthly meetings. The tribal council members are charged with representing the tribe in external matters during their tenure of three-year terms. Elections are staggered, and six officers are elected each spring at the June General Council meeting. All tribal members older than eighteen can vote, so long as they are present at General Council meetings. The General Council must approve any tribal measure that would affect the tribal constitution by a two-thirds' vote before the tribal council is able to execute such measures. The seat of power is in the hands of the Cowlitz people, and tribal council members are wise to take direction from the will of the General Council—or face loss at reelection in spring. Robin Torner, the vice chair of General Council in 2004, explains that all matters of the tribe,

> [l]egislative, executive and judicial, are handled by tribal council, at the pleasure of General Council. The "General Council" is a meeting of 250 to 400 or so members of the tribe who self-select themselves by physically showing up and thereby gaining voting rights for themselves on the day of the meeting. If you're a member of the tribe and you are present, you can speak and vote on any matter before the body, and often the meetings are somewhat scripted to pass constitutional amendments or motions sought by the tribal council for which the tribal council doesn't want to take full responsibility. All sorts of matters may be discussed and voted on but all things having to do with important policy making—e.g., fund-raising efforts, staffing levels, salaries, borrowing, lawsuits, political action, or specific program spending—will be kept off the agenda or speedily referred to the tribal council. (R. Torner 2005, 2)

Cowlitz General Council meetings roughly follow a business-meeting format, and the agenda is set by the Cowlitz Constitution. The meetings are frequently interrupted by long, spontaneous speeches, occasional outbursts, and various activities that stop the customary flow and pose a considerable challenge to *Robert's Rules of Order*. Children run in and out to see their parents, and elders leave as necessary to get a bite to eat or take care of other business. General Council meetings are important to Cowlitz tribal members, Torner (ibid.) explains, as many of them use this day to "register grievances, make announcements, get support for some special interest, and to get the latest news."

JOHN BARNETT, COWLITZ TRIBAL CHAIR

As chair of the General Council, Barnett is considered the chief and the official spokesman for the Cowlitz Tribe. Says Torner (ibid.): "As the constitution and bylaws are not specific as to the duties or powers of the officers, personality and enthusiasm are the only real limits on officer prerogatives." John Barnett was born in late 1934, well into the Great Depression. He was the son of an Indian father, Chippewa and Cowlitz, and a mother of full Finnish blood. His dad looked Indian and suffered for it, recalls Barnett (1989), at a time when the Columbia River area, where they lived, was populated with Europeans, many of them fair, blue-eyed Scandinavians. John's father labored as a lumberman, as did many men in the Pacific Northwest, working the forests and mills. When John was quite young, his parents divorced, and he moved with his mother to Seattle, where they resided through the war years, near the Bremerton shipping grounds. John, as do many of his generation, remembers the air raids and sirens blaring in the Puget Sound throughout this period.

His parents remarried when John was ten and relocated to Naselle, Washington, on the lower Columbia River. As a teenager and young man, John was an athlete. He attended college in the Northwest on an athletic scholarship. His family was poor, and the scholarship ensured that he could make it through school. He graduated from the College of Puget Sound in 1957 with a bachelor's degree in education. He taught for almost a dozen years before time and circumstance found him back in his ancestral occupation: the logging business. From his early thirties on, John struggled and at times prospered in this business. Also in his thirties, his engagement as a tribal official began.

The General Council meeting is an important day for the Cowlitz who attend; most people live some miles from Toledo and sometimes many states away from Washington, but on average two hundred to four hundred Cowlitz tribal members faithfully make the pilgrimage back once or twice a year, in June and November. Today, for the fall meeting, many participants have come to hear about the ICC's Docket 218, and the potential release of funds for tribal programming and elders. In the front of the room, in the center, amid the council members who sit facing the audience, is John. Today he makes the formal announcement about Docket 218.

Barnett's service as Cowlitz chair has a long history, one whose rules of deportment he is determined to uphold. As a child, he recalls, at General Council meetings in the 1930s and 1940s, the men in power, those able to sustain the focus and solidarity of the people, were men who were not afraid to speak up. The solemn women sat quietly at the side of the grange hall, legs crossed, but the men, says John, were apt to get up and perorate. "In those days the stature of an Indian was usually enhanced if he got up and gave a long speech over what had happened in the past, the wrongs and injustices" (Barnett 1989, 3). The more emotional the speech, the more it affected the groups' emotional members, sometimes leading to arguments among them. According to Barnett, speech making has a long history in the Cowlitz Tribe, and the members—especially the elders who have been attending these meetings for decades and watching the succession of chairmen—have come to expect strong words and strong leadership from their chairmen. Historically, the most effective Cowlitz chairmen have not been loathe to seize the stage to issue impassioned and controversial statements and foment conflict. In some cases, according to Barnett, to gain stature in the tribe a leader had to be willing to rouse anger and controversy among the people. The stronger the chairman's speech, explains Barnett (1989, 3), "the better chance he had to climb the ladder in the ranks of the Cowlitz tribe, and be respected."

"There weren't chiefs or subchiefs," he continues, "but [speech making] was a stature-building move. Indians in those days were noted for that. [Cowlitz chairman] James Sareault was an eloquent speaker with a loud, booming voice" (ibid.). Barnett's astute observation has suggestive links to past Coast Salish social and political organization. For instance, among the Quinault there were powerful and prominent men chosen by the chief to announce his intentions to the village and conduct negotiations with outsiders. These "speakers" were "chosen by the chief on the basis of qualifications such as a loud voice, ability to speak several languages and negotiating skills" (Hajda 1990, 510–11). Like many Cowlitz men, Barnett is big, well over six feet tall and long-legged. When he speaks, "there's no doubt who's in charge here" (quoted in Jacklet 1997, 13). His resonant voice is loud and easily surmounts any ambient noise in the room.

John almost never wears ribbon shirts or other objects sometimes identified with contemporary pan-Native movements. Nor does he favor the more traditional cedar clothing or accoutrements of Native people indigenous to the Pacific Northwest, although this would be rare in any case. In interviews he has mentioned that the Cowlitz men of his childhood frequently wore rounded, high cowboy hats, but John is almost always simply attired in pale blue chinos and a blue short-sleeved terry-cloth shirt that has just a bit of white accent. His brown leather shoes are comfortable, well broken in. His dark straight hair, white at the temples, is carefully combed in a side part, but everything else about his appearance is decidedly and emphatically unostentatious. Barnett could sit among the members, and—save for a certain high energy—blend in quite comfortably. He is economical in expression as well, quick-witted but laconic. The timber of his voice is something of a counterpoint to his unassuming demeanor; he can be absolutely commanding. In fact, he claims a reputation, "especially in the younger days," of being hotheaded. At contentious meetings throughout his decades-long history as tribal leader he has demonstrated that he doesn't fear conflict or even the occasional brawl.

As Barnett and other tribal historians have noted, there is a precedent in the tribe's long history of contention, and council meetings typically run all day. Sometimes meetings run for days, as people fight, figure things out, and wrangle over political issues and how to proceed. In matters of festival and event, everybody loves or at least fears a fight, but for the Cowlitz the conflict inherent in their public meetings has a demonstrable history and is part of an eventual consensus. However, this contention has caused trouble for the tribe in the eyes of the federal government, which frequently distrusts tribal factionalism rather than viewing it as potential gauge of community health and dynamism.[1]

The scholar Erving Goffman (1959 and 1974) has said that if part of the performance of self is being credible, then the audience's part in the performance is to be credulous. The successful performance relies on this dynamic, and Barnett is a most successful performer: he has the trust of his General Council members, by and large, because of his success in public political arenas and his persistence over time. Barnett has also ensured that the tenure of his leadership is made credible by its longevity: he has performed decades of service and has often made the sacrifices of time and money for the tribe—facts he is not afraid to mention. Such sacrifice is a well-recognized and respected tradition in the Cowlitz Tribe. As former tribal council chairman Robin Torner has noted, a leader has certain latitude within the Cowlitz Tribe, and so long as he adheres to the general ethos of the group and maintains decorum and trust under their scrutiny, he can go so far as his personal vision, resources, and drive will allow.

John Barnett is rich indeed in vision, resources, and drive. Together with many of the tribal council members who are deeply loyal to him and his mission, he has worked to make things better for the tribe. He has fought for fair treatment when he felt that the tribe had been swindled by the government in the settlement of Indian Claims in 1973. He has followed the process of federal acknowledgment from its beginning in 1978 and secured funding and offered his time and resources for its eventual success. Of course, not every Cowlitz agrees with Chairman Barnett, but most give their assent to his decisions. His manner is often brusque and dismissive, and his need for privacy and his concomitant need for personal control is keen and sometimes alienating. All of this can be observed in his discussion of Docket 218, where he relays a powerful narrative history for the tribe, both through "collective recollections" and "pedagogical" discourse. Barnett's rehearsal of this story is, in essence, a creation of the Cowlitz memory of landscape—a performance of their understanding of this genre.

THE ICC'S DECISION:
OUTSIDE CATEGORIES AND INSIDE CONFLICT

From the late 1940s, with the formation of the Indian Claims Commission, the Cowlitz Tribe fought for its land for some twenty-seven years. On April 12, 1973, the Cowlitz were awarded 1.5 million dollars for 1.66 million acres of land, based on a "date of taking" of March 20, 1863. Upon this reward, after nearly three decades of struggle, the Bureau of Indian Affairs (BIA) withheld the judgment funds for another thirty-one years. For the Cowlitz people, the memory of the settlement decision and its meager award still stings. The lack of substantive compensation, government mismanagement of meetings surrounding the claim decision, and the insult of having to "take it" lingers in John Barnett's memory. Of the decision he says bitterly: "Yeah, but then the federal government said that all other rights belong with the land, rights and ownership of the land. And that's how they stripped us of the land. And that's how they stripped us of our hunting and fishing rights" (Barnett 2003a, 5–8). Though some tribal peoples were content to receive the Docket 218 dispensation, Barnett, vice chairman of the General Council in 1973, was emphatically not among them.

He regrets the loss of land use rights for gaming and for fishing, as much as anything else. In 1973 he and others, though continuing their relationship with the Cowlitz Tribe proper, broke from the main and formed a group called the Sovereign Cowlitz. This group would last only a short while but stood powerfully against the demonstrable injustice in land settlement at the hands of the federal government. It was, in part, the Sovereign Cowlitz's forceful disagreement with the government that led to the government's decision to hold Docket 218 funds in escrow until the Cowlitz Tribe secured federal acknowledgment. As mentioned, however, there was (and still is) an internal precedent of dissent for the Cowlitz Tribe that goes back many years. Meetings were heated and full of arguments. In fact, the stronger and more emotional a chairman could be, the more potent his speech in affective content, the more likely he was to persuade the group to cohere and move forward. Such impassioned leadership, according to Barnett, enhanced the clout of the chairman. In 1973, the heated debate between those who felt the land claims release was a sham and those who felt the Cowlitz ought to settle might have been resolved given that debate was the culturally relevant way the community traditionally righted itself. The debate might have been resolved if the community dynamic had been allowed to play itself out. Instead, in perhaps the worst of outcomes, the government asserted its own interpretation of "ownership."

In his fieldwork with island Hul'quminum, scholar Brian Thom (2005, 214) has demonstrated that the "ways that place names and their stories are used to articulate ideas of territories, particularly in the context of contemporary land claims" will more often than not "muddle notions of exclusive territories as conceived in western legal traditions, and reveal part of the complex relationships of sharing that underlie the social, economic fabric of Coast Salish communities." In a cogent observation regarding the "trustworthiness" of Native testimony, tribal member Robin Torner (2005, 1) says: "It's interesting that the problem [of Native definition] persists today in newspapers where citizens are claiming the Cowlitz has no 'geographical right' to [trust land] where it wants to build, and the tribe claims it has an 'ancestral' right. The argument will undoubtedly be left to the ethnohistorians of both sides. What the Indians say themselves will be dismissed as self-serving, as it always was." If Native testimony is considered "self-serving" and otherwise grossly distorted in matters regarding resource distribution, then whose testimony is admissible?

The Cowlitz's claim to their own voice and agency often centers on a claim to their land and, by extension, tribal identity. Landedness, in light of Docket 218, is very vulnerable. The fragility here rests in an ambiguous authority of the state over its Indian subjects, but this fragility has preceded state rule. For the tribal chairman the ideal is to protect the tribe as a unit, as positively bounded, so the federal agents who occasionally look in and define the group will not feel compelled to take the Cowlitz Indian Tribe's hard won land and title away. In interviews and at council meetings, Chairman Barnett frequently evokes the past as an outrage. He holds the government's past actions as evidence of Cowlitz survival against all odds: how they endured and ultimately prevailed, and how they will again. During the meeting of 1973, called by the government, Barnett resisted passionately. He remembers:

To me, it was an insult. I spoke very strongly against the acceptance.... There was a core group of probably fifteen of us who were very much opposed to the accepting of such a slap-in-the-face offer by the federal government. The thing that bothered me at the meeting was that there were people standing up—and you knew they were there to vote on something and it didn't matter whether it was a five-dollar check or a five-hundred-dollar check, they simply wanted that check. As an example, I remember one lady standing up and saying, "I want my money. I don't care if it is just enough to buy a new refrigerator. I want my money." The amount didn't matter. What they wanted was to receive something for what they thought was nothing. They did not fully realize the impact of the issue at hand. I looked at the compensation as something that was rightfully ours and it should have been a just amount that was offered. And it was not. (Barnett 2002, 7)

In many respects, as vice chairman of Cowlitz General Council, Barnett took the moral high ground in 1973. From his perspective, looking back in time, the Docket 218 dispensation was not about the check, it was about the principle. Resistance was necessary to preserve Cowlitz dignity. "There was no thought of getting the land back," he says, "but of getting justice for what they had lost, because many of them still had land—in some cases trust land, but in other cases tracts of land or homesteads as we knew homesteads in those days. Many people owned land, but had been pushed off . . . or forced out" (ibid., 2). Barnett's perspective is that he was only trying to do what was best, to ask for a fair price and a fair process for his people. The initial offer of some sixty-five cents an acre and the eventual price of ninety-three cents an acre was, he thinks, a raw deal. Some Cowlitz decided they must continue to fight. The government answered by ignoring the traditional vernacular of the Cowlitz Tribe, which had a precedent in consensus through dissent. There was evidence to point to Cowlitz cohesion in 1973, despite the existence of factions.

During the entire period when there was contention over Docket 218 distribution, Barnett held office for the tribe. He says: "It seems ironic that at that time I was vice chair of the Sovereign Cowlitz Tribe, and the vice chair for the Cowlitz Tribe of Indians" (ibid., 9). Nevertheless, the government felt that factionalism was evidence enough to suggest that the tribe itself was not able to handle the land award coming to it. Their decision seems questionable, given that the Cowlitz had held together since an agreed date of 1863, and prior, under worse and more adversarial circumstances. Says Barnett:

> I think the government has used that fact to its own advantage today to show there was a split in the Cowlitz Tribe. But it wasn't a split in the Cowlitz Tribe. It wasn't a split in the thinking inside of us as being Cowlitz Indians. It was a split in the point of view about our treatment by the federal government by the offer of that compromise settlement and the subsequent continuation to uphold it through the hearing in Tacoma and then the two meetings on Cowlitz Prairie. We were still Cowlitz Indians, but we did not wish to sell our aboriginal homeland for $1,550,000. (Ibid., 10)

In this history, and in this context, John Barnett stands as chairman of the Cowlitz Tribe thirty-one years later, in November 2004, to make a historic announcement to the elders: they have finally received financial award from Docket 218. Per agreement with the government, the elders have received checks in compensation.[2] The rest of the financial award will be distributed as a percentage of its investment earning over the past three decades, to such tribal programs as education, elderly assistance, emergency assistance, natural resources, housing assistance, and health. Barnett announces the remarkable news at the meeting, saying: "This is the historical day, this is the day Docket 218 is released." He asks the elders to rise and acknowledge acceptance of their Docket 218 checks. They stand. Many are in tears, as are those watching. All are applauding.

MOUNTAIN OF RESENTMENT

Roy Wilson (1988, 1), the Cowlitz spiritual elder, once said of Chairman Barnett that when he spoke using nature metaphors, he became a "powerful man of the earth." The land of southwestern Washington means and has always meant something to Barnett and his people. He was willing to risk everything and fight the government over it. Like many Cowlitz people,

Barnett envisions Cowlitz ties to the land as existing since time immemorial. "Time immemorial" is a term used commonly among Native Americans to describe the occupation of their homeland, a place that predates any contact with outsiders. According to Judith Irwin, a historian who has worked with the Cowlitz since the early 1970s, the core of Salish and Cowlitz identity is related to their longtime residence on the land in southwestern Washington. "Where one was born, grew up, married, has chosen to live," she wrote, matters more than "blood quantum, language, or cultural mores" in defining a core Cowlitz identity (J. Irwin 1994, 50). "Loyalty to the Cowlitz country, the land or ancestral area," she explains, is a key means by which Cowlitz people claim their sense of group identity and emplacement (ibid., 50).

In his influential and beautifully rendered book *Wisdom Sits in Places*, anthropologist Keith Basso speaks to the profound implications of place and evocation of place by a community of people, in this instance the Western Apache. Words of place convey worlds, and there is a clear relationship between the word and the place that is second nature to the Native that an anthropologist might miss. Given the growing importance of land to human survival, this is a relationship that should be understood. The features of landscape "acquire value and significance by virtue of the ideational systems with which they are apprehended and construed" (Basso 1996, 72). The anthropologist Michael Roe (2003, 70–71), who has worked specifically with the Cowlitz, says that "the Cowlitz's intimacy with the land can be interpreted as a construction of their past which does emphasize unity, and so conceivably fits within Lyons's group cohesion criteria [of social memory]; it is also, however, a very real experience in their present [and] can be described as continuity . . . in the present." Cowlitz attachment to the land is neither abstract nor idle. "Land . . . is indispensable to the economic and social well-being of a tribal people," writes anthropologist Ken Tollefson (1996, 321, quoted in Roe 2003, 55); "dislocated tribal people generally seek some tangible estate in order to maintain their common fund and their system of values."

As the applause dies down in the meeting hall, and the elders settle back into their seats, Barnett takes the microphone in hand. He resumes his chairman's report: "In 1980 Mount Saint Helens blew," he intones, referring to the famous volcanic eruption; "I believe it was due to the actions of the government and our neighbors." The phrases "actions of the government" and "actions of our neighbors" erase the divide separating 1980 and the present. These actions are inextricably linked to the present and to the mountain's actual eruption. Each speaks to a historic tribal anger, similar to the chair's own history of anger. Barnett then refers the Cowlitz audience to other events of 1980, when the Cowlitz Tribe filed with the Wahkiakum Chinook in a cooperative litigation for the right to fish on the Columbia and Cowlitz Rivers. Eventually, in 1981, the Ninth Circuit Court of Appeals reaffirmed a post-treaty affiliation of the Chinook and Cowlitz, allowing them to fish but only on Quinault land. Recalls Barnett (1989, 15): "We watched the outcome of the Boldt decision [in 1974] and saw how the recognized tribes got rights to certain ceded areas in which they had fished. [We] were Indians. We were denied the right to fish in our aboriginal areas. What is good for one tribe as a right to fish should be good for all."[3]

Barnett was displeased with this outcome, as were Roy Wilson and other Cowlitz. In discussing the mountain in a clear connection to the outcome of the Wahkiakum case, Barnett evokes a tribal, group anger. He says: "The language was to the effect that, through post-treaty affiliation, the Chinook and the Cowlitz are entitled to all the rights and benefits of the actual signatories of the Treaty of Olympia within the ceded area of that treaty. That in a sense the Chinook and Cowlitz cannot fish the Columbia or the Cowlitz Rivers, but that they are entitled to a fishing right within the Treaty of Olympia. [This] is the bad part of our judicial system that on the local level politics plays more a part in decision making, regardless of what the law says, than people realize" (Barnett 1989, 15–16). People sit rapt, listening as Barnett sets up the story of Mount Saint Helens. "In 2004 there's a new [lava] dome, and it's consistent with the growth of the Cowlitz Indian Tribe. Our own Indianness, our own initiative. We have learned how to manage things and how to survive!" (ibid.). The Cowlitz have a long history with the mountain. Precontact, they lived at its base and traversed around it, though reputedly none would walk up the mountain because they believed it possessed evil spirits.

Barnett is particularly alert today, especially animated, and he is speaking to the tribe in a manner they well recognize; it's a story they have heard before, of how the tribe has survived all things and stood together. "The dome of Saint Helens is building," he intones, referring to the mountain's new growth in recent years. "Don't lose sight. There is much more to come. Be patient, for there will be many more benefits for you and your families and children. It's about our people." As he says this, Barnett's voice cracks with emotion, although his face remains impassive: "We've learned how to manage things to survive," he says, "on a little pittance . . . a little pittance of sixty-five cents an acre. [In] 1863 our land was taken, open to homesteaders and yet we're still here. We've always been here, and we refuse to move" (ibid.).

In his speech the reduction in the mountain is a result of the government's bad behavior (the disappointing natural resource decision by the Ninth Circuit Court of Appeals regarding Cowlitz fishing rights), which metaphorically represents a reduction in the Cowlitz tribe. An accretion in the mountain, in the present, indicates an increase for the Cowlitz (because they have learned to manage their own affairs) in the future. The chairman's discussion of past, present, and future indicates that the past was one of depletion and dependence. The present is one of accretion, and the future promises to be a happy one (as the claims are disbursed to elders and will ultimately be disbursed to Cowlitz administrative programs), but only if the Cowlitz remember what they have learned and their past. The mountain, whether depleted or growing, is at all times equivalent to the Cowlitz people. The mountain is ancient. It precedes the loss of land, it survives all maps and global positioning systems and historical records. If the Cowlitz young can remember the mountain, then that memory of time beyond time will serve their patience and eventually yield vindication—if not for them, then for *their* children.

The call for "patience" and a refusal to move are recurring themes for Barnett. He summons all of tribal history to this very day in November, urging General Council members to keep faith in the tribe, especially at this auspicious moment when recognition is cast, Docket 218 is flowing, and the future looks bright. He reminds them to stay the course, as the Cowlitz Tribe has been doing since "time immemorial," a pivotal phrase for Barnett and other tribal leaders. "Time precontact" is when the Cowlitz people remained whole and were safe upon the land. "Time immemorial" can be seen in geologic time as well as in "natural" time, a different sort of temporality that outpaces the more short-term memory of the postcontact world. Barnett summons this mythic time often. In his reckoning, the tribe is very much like Mount Saint Helens: strong, enduring, and powerful. The tribe, like the mountain, existed prior to white contact and it will continue to exist.

Yet Cowlitz attachment to the land is much more than a hearkening to an Edenic past, in which all things are thought to be in balance and in harmony with the "circle of life." Likening Mount Saint Helens to the Cowlitz Tribe is more than a pretty metaphor summoned by Chairman Barnett as he addresses his people; it is a metaphor that speaks to and reasserts the Cowlitz people's firm attachment to the land, their understanding of their history in southwestern Washington, and their historical engagement with the federal government. The volcanic imagery summons and evokes their anger at the series of injustices the tribe has endured. It is a potent and regionally located metaphor of permanence for the dispossessed, but the Cowlitz, who have lived in the foothills near Saint Helens for millennia, have a relationship to the mountain that is substantively different from their white neighbors.

THE IMPORTANCE OF PLACE-NAMES

Mount Saint Helens sits in a volcanic chain among other young, rugged, and vividly beautiful mountains in the Cascade Range in the Pacific Northwest. Saint Helens has been erupting for at least ten thousand years, with explosive intervals separated by as many as five thousand years and as few as a hundred. It was especially active from 1831 to the late 1850s, when settlers new to the area reported seeing steam plumes and other volcanic activity. Father Jean Baptiste Zacharie Bolduc reported seeing the peak erupt in 1843 while he was staying with Catholic priests Demers and Blanchet at the mission that was once and is now Cowlitz property in Toledo, Washington.

The eruption on May 18, 1980, at 8:32 A.M. was enormous. It completely blew apart the peak's northern flank and sent a lethal blast of hot gas, steam, and rock debris sweeping across the landscape at speeds as fast as 683.5 miles per hour, thrusting a giant plume of ash miles into the sky, where it was carried on the wind to land all over the western United States.

There is no underestimating the significance of the explosion to communities in western Oregon and Washington, but the importance here is not upon popular imagination but rather upon personal imagination as it is revealed in Barnett's summoning of a place whose meaning is particular to him and his tribe. Claiming it, as Barnett does, as a mnemonic for Cowlitz anger is a far-reaching claim.

The name for the mountain currently called Saint Helens was known as Sa Kw in Lower Cowlitz. Its name in Upper Cowlitz (Taidnapam), a dialect of Sahaptin, was Lawilayt, which translates as "the smoker." This indicates to me that Lawilayt/Sa Kw was well understood by the Cowlitz for quite some time for its most salient action. If we believe, as do many who study Native use of place-names, that Sahaptin place-names refer to *where things happen*, then it makes sense that for an undesignated but presumably significant amount of time, the thing that happened at Saint Helens was steam or eruption. Given that the mountain erupts at intervals of anywhere from one hundred to five thousand years and that the last series of eruptions to occur with any frequency would have been in 1830, when the Sahaptin designation for Mount Saint Helens was Lawilayt, we can assume that this name has a long and likely ancient history.

"The features of the local landscape," claims Keith Basso (1996, 72), "no less than utterances exchanged in daily discourse, acquire value and significance by virtue of the ideational systems with which they are apprehended and construed." In the Cowlitz people's estimation, their land was stolen, yet they remain. The scholar Ward Churchill (1993, 4) has asserted that "recognition of the legal and moral rights by which a nation occupies its land base is a fundamental issue of its existence," not to be conflated with an essentialism that collapses "Native regard of the land into a spiritual environmentalism." It is imperative that scholars studying Native communities understand the fundamental link between Native community and place. Place is not merely the inert ground, inviolable and permanent, upon which a group stands, builds, and forges community. It is itself a fluid and interpretable entity, and the manner in which the Cowlitz characterize Saint Helens reveals something about their "conceptions of reality, [and] the meanings of the landscapes" (Basso 1996, 72). Members of a local community, writes Basso (ibid., 73), "involve themselves in their geographical landscape in at least three distinct ways": through observation, use of, and communication about the landscape. In the last mode, explains Basso, "communicative acts of topographic representation—will be most revealing of the conceptual instruments with which Native people interpret their natural surroundings," and although "such representations may be fashioned from a variety of semiotic materials (gestural, pictorial, musical, and others), few are more instructive than those which are wrought with words."

The very dispossession and divestment of the Cowlitz from their landscape make the evocation of Saint Helens particularly telling. The anthropologist Jon Daehnke has grappled with issues of tribal dispossession and divestment from the land in his consideration of the Confluence Project, a series of monuments erected on the Columbia River to commemorate the Lewis and Clark Bicentennial and intended to involve tribal voices and stories. The project instead managed to "assimilate the Native American story as one more component of the American master narrative, create a false equation of Indigenous and settler experiences on the landscape," and hide a "specific history of colonial violence and dispossession" by presenting an "ahistorical story of shared environmental concerns" (Daehnke 2012, 503). Far from inhabiting their space and place in an uneventful series of eons, the Cowlitz have been removed and returned to this site at Saint Mary's Mission any number of times and in any number of ways where, from any north-facing window, they look out on a stunning view of Mount Saint Helens, weather permitting. Since 2002, the Cowlitz have been "officially" back upon this land, and their purchase guarantees that they may lay claim to it, as they restore land base and come together as a community.

A close consideration of Chair Barnett's Saint Helens speech reveals tropes of resistance, subsistence, and conflation of the Cowlitz Tribe with the natural landscape. The use of nature imagery bolsters his claims for the tribe. The tribe is like the mountain: strong, enduring, and ever adapting to as well as imposing change upon the environment. A mountain outlasts its adversaries. Barnett and the Cowlitz people he leads have legitimate anger and, like the volcano, they contain a subterranean explosive quality, a potential. They have a way of showing the outside world that their power is increasing, their flow is rising, and their anger is mighty. On the day of Docket 218's release, the Cowlitz are acknowledging themselves and their history in this place. On this day they are recognizing and receiving recognition; money for their land is a potent, if bitter, recognition. They are being released: with Saint Helens's release, as it rises and builds its dome, so the Cowlitz people build with cash a comeuppance.

DWELLING AND DOING:
THE POETICS OF COWLITZ ATTACHMENT TO THE LAND

In his use of a place-name, Chairman Barnett exemplifies strength of leadership and demonstrates his priorities for the group. It is always fruitful to pay close attention to those individuals in a group who bear witness to their group's history and to the wider historical milieu in which that history takes place. They describe and bring to full articulation what is felt by many engaged in the group's community life. It is important to ask, however, whether other Cowlitz people speak of an attachment to land. The answer to that is, yes, they most certainly do.

Historian Judith Irwin (1979 and 1994), who has worked with the Cowlitz for many years, notes that for the Cowlitz, where one grew up and stayed tends to matter more than other identity markers, such as blood quantum. It is very important to the Cowlitz, she says, to remain loyal to "Cowlitz country" and their aboriginal territory. Darleen Fitzpatrick (1986) concurs: for the Cowlitz a key component of their ethnic identity is their attachment to the land of southwestern Washington. Although the Cowlitz have maintained their identity in part because they have remained on their usual and accustomed land in southwestern Washington, there is more to this observation than might at first meet the eye. If "place" is more a consideration of human connection that mere space, what can be said of Cowlitz locality that tells us more about the nature of their relationship to the land and its importance for the continuity of group and belonging?

Anthropologist Brian Thom (2000, 2005, and 2006) has studied the Coast Salish people's relationship between language, culture, and individual influence. He has found that attachment to home places is the foundation of Coast Salish people's orientation to both self and culture. Thom claims that Coast Salish people do not approach their "environment as an external world that has to be grasped conceptually and conceptualized symbolically within the terms of an imposed cultural design as a precondition for effective action. Indeed the separation of mind and nature has no place in their thought and practice" (Thom 2005, 25). While Western notions of land and territory tend to rest on narrow conceptions of economy and strict management of space as a place that shapes bodily habit and movement, Thom has found that the Coast Salish people with whom he worked tended to see relationships between economies and activity as seamless and not bounded by narrower conceptions of place and state. For many Native peoples, in fact, places are lived in and experienced in a seamless fashion that reconciles (or does not experience) the division made in Western thought and experience between nature and culture. Thom calls this "dwelling"—a term that serves as a verbal shorthand for the complex interplay of locality, place, and the imagination that creates a sense of belonging and attachment to the land.

For Native people, Thom notes, daily life is characterized by relationship to the land and the creatures that dwell in it. It is a life in which one "cares for, respects, and exchanges power with the land and other beings"; as a result, "property becomes organized by and reflects back into these cultural systems and practices" (Thom 2005, 28). Like Thom, ethnographer Julie Cruikshank (1998, 20–22) has also thought about place and the relationship Native peoples have to it. In her important work *The Social Life of Stories*, she argues that Western and state conceptions of land are called into question by Native ontologies, in which world views are reflected in narratives of place. In a discussion about elders in the Yukon and their conflict with the state over land ownership and land divisions, Cruikshank (ibid., 16–17) writes:

> If elders speak of language as reflecting multilingualism and communication, they speak of land in terms of travel and mobility, frequently constructing life stories as travel narratives. Their understanding of land ownership rarely includes formal boundaries. . . . Community land claims negotiators, on the other hand, face the difficult task of reconciling the state's narratives about land as bounded units to be owned. [Native women involved in state negotiation say,] "You know, I think it's all the same thing. People are starting to think about their identity, about who they are. And you know how it is when you start thinking about who you are—right way, you think of *place*."

For both Thom and Cruikshank, the important idea is that "property" and "territory" are congruent with more symbolic notions of space for Native (i.e., the Coast Salish and Yukon) peoples. But is this so for the Cowlitz? Do the Cowlitz express their attachment to land in terms of dwelling upon it? Do they express or reflect their identity by means of attachment to the land?

Michael Roe (2003) has worked as an academic researcher with the Cowlitz since 1981. He discusses the importance of a land base to the Cowlitz people. Roe was among those academics involved in the mid-1990s (during the Cowlitz's work for federal recognition) in a modern community study component of the federal acknowledgment process. He found that the research domains of "social interaction" and "ethnic identity" were especially compelling as indicators of continuity of Cowlitz identity from past (precontact) to present (modern community). In his research, Roe concluded that Cowlitz engagement with the federal government has led to an "entrenchment" or buckling down of their identity and that this persistence of identity was especially apparent when it came to Cowlitz perceptions of their land, spirituality, and connection to their ancestors. Roe said that the Cowlitz connection to the land demonstrated their continuity as a people, linking them to the past and continuing in the present.

Furthermore, Roe (2003, 66) concluded that Cowlitz survival and identity-making was contingent upon "social memories" that fed the "context and content" of what would be remembered later. His conception of Cowlitz modern identity and attachment to land rests on the central tenet that continuity of the Cowlitz group can only be demonstrated by "constructions of the past," noting that Cowlitz people relate their identity to their ancestry. I wonder if Roe's conclusion about Cowlitz identity—premised as it is on historical notions of the past as a construction—tends to reassert dominant Western categories of thought that preclude or tend to obscure indigenous understandings. It is true that the Cowlitz have resisted the federal government and have gained much of their contemporary identity and infused much of their contemporary rhetoric with a vision of "us" against "them," a people against the state. But is it not also true that individual efforts to sustain Cowlitz culture may take yet another form, apart from the assertion that their collective memory is formed in large part by a resistance to the state?

Fitzpatrick, who conducted her lengthy study with the Cowlitz in the early 1980s, uses the phrase "salience of ethnicity" to denote times when a person's understanding of ethnic identity surfaces because he or she has experienced or remembered some event or thing that brings to the fore an identification with his or her ethnic identity. Fitzpatrick (1986, 336) says that "social recognition and salience of ethnicity occur due to experiences, circumstances, times and events that call to mind an ethnic identity." While she doesn't deal with either genres of landscape per se or their symbolic function, she does outline the circumstances in which "salience" seems to occur for her subjects. "Cowlitz ties to the land and the historical and cultural ramifications are strongly expressed in their remarks," Fitzpatrick writes, again locating the Cowlitz discourse in terms of history and culture. She goes on to say that: "Cowlitz spoke in my interviews with them about the ancestral area as a necessary feature of the ethnicity of the group and about the historical events that resulted in the dispossession of those lands. Twice I was told that the Cowlitz are similar to the Palestinians who want to live in their ancestral lands" (ibid., 260). Fitzpatrick draws her observations from interviews with the Cowlitz people, in which they discuss residence upon the Cowlitz River and endurance on the area's land and hold provocative discussions of land usage, such as when they mention prairie burning, which was a millennia-old practice among southwestern Washington aboriginal peoples. The cues and clues in the interviews often point to an alternate reason as to why remaining on Cowlitz land was an important part of their identity.

Like Roe, Fitzpatrick uses compelling firsthand material from the Cowlitz people to conclude that it is the history and the past that evoke "salience" and a provocation of ethnic identity for them. She says that "we are acquainted enough with Cowlitz history during contact time to know that from at least 1850 to the end of the century, Cowlitz experienced removal and were steadily divested of their aboriginal land holdings" (ibid., 263–65). But this seems to miss the point. It is neither the pursuit of land nor history alone that evokes salience, although these undoubtedly do create and secure meaning among the Cowlitz. What I found in my research is that although ancestral area and remaining upon it is a priority for many Cowlitz people, it is also the attendant activity upon their ancestral land and the manner in which they consider that activity that prompts a lively remembering and language of belonging. Actual life upon the land, subsistence upon it, and interaction with it serve as indicators of a vibrant Cowlitz identity, existing independently of narratives of resistance to the state and historical relationships to aboriginal territory that rely upon the strict demarcations of usual and accustomed territory as defined by and negotiated with outsiders.

Fitzpatrick does, however, approach the idea that Cowlitz attachment to the land is not merely symbolic. She notes that an attachment to the land produced in her Cowlitz subjects a deep feeling that moved beyond the symbolic realm into the affective realm. Of elder Joe Cloquet, a past chairman and leader of the tribe, she writes: "Joe Cloquet, an Upper Cowlitz approaching the status of an elder, speaks about 'getting a funny feeling' when he drives through Olequa where his father's family is from.... [H]is descent from Cowlitz ancestors and his ties to the land area are symbolic.... Olequa stimulates a certain kind of feeling in him [and] the town is acting in an indexical mode. He did not say—when I hear the word Olequa I get a 'funny *kind of* feeling'—as he would if the town were purely a symbol to him" (Fitzpatrick 1986, 256–57).

Fitzpatrick (ibid., 57) adds: "I think his response tells us how important it is to the Cowlitz to locate their office and base of operations in the Cowlitz aboriginal area since the meaning of the land acts upon them in ways that are not merely symbolic." She persists in her claim, however, that the Cowlitz continue to emphasize, if not define, ethnicity by residence on the aboriginal land area. Fitzpatrick does not press her analysis to consider the contemporary Cowlitz activity and engagement with the land, nor what the narratives describing this activity can tell us about Cowlitz priorities. She says "that the people are to the land as history is to the traditional customs because much of traditional Cowlitz culture is no longer practiced" (ibid., 258). This assumption, in keeping with Western paradigms of possession and dispossession, holds that the Cowlitz are no longer attached to the land and hence there is loss rather than continuity or renewal. Fitzpatrick defines the relationship in terms of an absent or lost land; she fails to address what is present before her: even if the Cowlitz members do not have a land base, they maintain activities that they experience as inherently Cowlitz, inherently real, upon the land of their ancestors. Hence, her analysis remains in the realm of recollection, nostalgia, and history to describe Cowlitz salience of ethnicity. Lived events can also evoke and make Cowlitz ethnicity salient in Cowlitz people.

Roe's and Fitzpatrick's analyses focus on Cowlitz attachment to the land and the fact that the Cowlitz are landless. Each researcher concludes that landlessness is the focus of Cowlitz loss, tenacity, and anger: qualities that work to keep them bound by common experience and together as a group. In my observation this is certainly true. However, I suggest the complementary idea that the Cowlitz people are simultaneously using and inhabiting the land. If we adhere to Thom's and Cruikshank's assertions that Native conceptions of attachment to the land are ones of *belonging to the world*, how might we arrive at different conclusions for Cowlitz salience of ethnicity, group continuity, and strength of identity, and in what light can we consider these activities and the ideas surrounding them?

We now have a framework with which to discuss the Cowlitz interviews by a consideration of ways of being on the land, or "dwelling." This term that allows us to listen to the Cowlitz experience upon the land as one that does not always rely upon predefined and polarized relationships between nature and culture, a common division in Western thought that is used to structure space and experience in specific ways that accord with the state's values and presuppose a more distanced and demarcated relationship between what is "land" and what is not. Let us now consider what my interviews with Cowlitz tribal members about attachment to the land reveal about Cowlitz priorities.

THE INTERVIEWS: "DOING" INDIAN

Most of the interviews took place from 1997 to 2004. In many informal discussions, e-mail exchanges, and interviews, I came to find that these Cowlitz people frequently expressed a connection of being Native to activities done on Cowlitz usual and accustomed territory. The interviews included here are with Cowlitz subjects whom I would define as active members of the tribe: those who serve on committees and as politicians and who regularly attend General Council and other Cowlitz functions. The subjects range in age from mid-thirties to mid-sixties.

Because I heard time and again the passion with which fellow Cowlitz lived upon the land—whether it be hunting, fishing, camping, digging clams, or harvesting seasonal foods—I became captivated with the manner in which descriptions of their "life outside" seemed a close companion to their solid attachment to Cowlitz ethnicity and identity. I considered for a long while how to ask in a formal fashion what it was like "to be outside." What it was like to camp. What it was like to fish, hunt, smelt, or dig for clams. What it was like to know the native plants of the area and when to harvest them. But there was more to the question, I sensed, than the mechanics of a particular act. For when the Cowlitz people discussed these activities, by and large there was an attendant pride and sense of enhanced "Indianness" that accompanied the discussion.

Thus I was led to ask a simple question of my interviewees that yielded a rich answer: How do you "do" Indian? By this I meant two things: what activities did they associate with their Native identity, if any; and what was it about these activities that evoked "salience," a clear sense of seeing and identifying with their Native identity? To "do" Indian also referred to the bodily practices and spatial use that complements Thom's "dwelling" and Cruikshank's "categories of belonging." The Cowlitz relationship to nature suggested a seamlessness that complicated the nature-culture divide. The ways in which my Cowlitz interviewees described their activities (formally to me and informally among themselves) called to mind the manner in which activity and narrative can smooth potential rupture (in this case, the rupture of being both divested of the land and yet belonging to the land). I asked my question either in person or by correspondence. Most of the interviewees responded with great interest and exhibited no real hesitation at my question's potential awkwardness of phrase.[4]

Being a Native American is one thing, and being a Native who characterizes himself and his tribe as historically landless tells us something significant about potential sources of tribal identity, but the idea of "doing Native" and the nature of what is done tells us more, and tells us in more precise terms, about attachment to the land. Through interviews with Cowlitz tribal members, I found three recurring priorities: entitlement, resourcefulness, and "being (and doing) Indian." "Entitlement" refers to the double meaning of both holding a title to the land and a sense that one is *entitled* to be upon and use land for his purposes, regardless of title. "Resourcefulness" alludes to resources as being something that are—in the Western imagination—either renewable or nonrenewable and serve primarily as a means to amass wealth. The meaning of "resources" for Cowlitz generally reflects a relationship to the land and its bounty that provides a living—both spiritual and corporeal. "Being (and doing) Indian" refers to the frequency with which interviewees would say that acting upon the land evoked a clear sense of connection to one's inherent Indian nature and to his or her family and ancestors. Together, these three priorities form a cohesive whole that I call "doing Indian."

To "do Indian" refers to bodily practice and spatial use upon one's ancestral land, as distinct from a stubborn remaining upon the land. "Doing Indian" is active. In interviews with Cowlitz tribal members, I found continuity among their descriptions of how they inhabit and conceive of their relationship to Cowlitz land and resources. This continuity points to Cowlitz priorities that provide an efficacious and meaningful tribal identification that helps to strengthen both individual identity and provide for the possibility of a Cowlitz collective identity. With remarkable frequency interviewees would say that acting upon the land evoked a clear sense of connection to one's inherent Indian nature and to his or her family and ancestors. Resistance to the white man's laws and a sense that one is entitled to be upon and use land for his purposes, regardless of title, often came up. The meaning of "resources" for the Cowlitz interviewed often reflected a relationship of use with natural resources by an individual to provide subsistence. Cowlitz connection to the land's resources leads to a deep sense of spiritual connection, both to the land and to Cowlitz family and ancestors.

The interviewees expressed an entitlement to be upon the land and to use the land's resources regardless of boundaries, restrictions, and rules of the state. Robin Torner tells a compelling story of how the woods are so dense and deep that few game wardens can follow one who does not wish to be found. Even when restrictions were created to regulate hunting and fishing, Torner says, "there was no concerted organized effort by tribal leaders to defeat the game wardens once and for all [, instead], every family simply 'took up poaching' in violation of what the Indians knew were foolish and unnecessary restrictions on their traditional hunting and fishing," and although they had to exercise caution, violating state rule proved to be fairly straightforward. As Torner (2004, 1) notes, "the woods are deep and the river runs in remote places . . . and the "Cowlitz violate hunting and fishing rules to this day, and will until their traditional rights are recognized and upheld by the State and Federal government."

Robin Torner has hunted since he was twelve years old, and although he once made it a point to teach others, he now prefers to hunt alone. "I just go and do it," he says, "my time, my woods, my way," emphasizing the joy he takes in merging with the land. "I enjoy it because alone I make up my own rules as to method and bag limit. The State laws don't enter into it and so I'm free from the State, too" (ibid., 2). Torner feels a sense of liberation when he is out in the woods alone, not necessarily making up new rules but reinstating what he considers to be the proper way of being in the woods and selecting carefully from its bounty. "My woods, my way," he says, reflecting what it feels like when he feels most connected to his Native heritage. "When I'm out in the forests, alone," he explains, "it's usually just me and the woods as it was before the settlers turned hunting—a noble, necessary function of life—into a perverted blood sport. Actually, they turned it into a circus. The clowns dress up in [a] blaze of orange. . . . I just go pick up whatever presents itself as I need . . . where God put it for me in the seasons He set; not the State Wildlife Commission" (ibid., 2). Torner clearly identifies himself apart from "the settlers" and the state, better aligned with a spiritual source reflecting his own sense of what it means to a Cowlitz man: dwelling upon and using the land and its bounty intelligently and selectively and not for blood sport (ibid., 2).

For many Cowlitz their identity as hunters and fishers is enduring, an important part of how they think of themselves as being in the world. Earlier in this chapter, we saw how Chairman John Barnett traced history back to the inadequate results of the Wahkiakum fish case; the Cowlitz's inability to legally fish the Cowlitz River (or even the Columbia River) is an affront, a source of sadness and even outrage for some Cowlitz people. Nearly every Cowlitz person I interviewed, old and young alike, prides himself on being able to live off the land as a hunter or fisher. A common story among Cowlitz people centers on the "fish-ins" of the 1960s and 1970s. My own family loves to talk about Great Grandma Rose, who fished for Steelhead, Coho, and Chinook salmon well into her eighties. When Washington State law threatened to curtail Rose's habit of fishing whenever she felt like it, she secreted salmon into her hip-high waders to avoid the strictures of the game warden.

The Cowlitz see themselves as a river-dwelling people, and the salmon is sacred to them. They have for many years been politically motivated to protect salmon resources. As early as the 1950s, Robin Torner (1994, 22) notes, "the Cowlitz Indian Tribe [was] the only dissenter to a proposal to dam the Cowlitz River for hydroelectric power. The tribe's opposition was rooted in concern that a dam would diminish the natural salmon runs." The tribe's "worst fears" were born out, Torner (ibid.) claims, for although in "1950 public concern for salmon stocks was not the political issue it is today, the environmental science we have now, while hardly complete, is certainly strong enough to vindicate the tribe's view of 1950. That they were not listened to at this point marks the steady decline of this once enormously productive salmon watershed."

For those who do fish or hunt according to state law, there is a sense of loss. "Fishing like white men" is clearly in opposition to a Native identity. Cowlitz members Julie Klein and her brother, Bob Bouchard, reflected on this issue:

JULIE: Being Indian is more about quality than quantity (in relation to blood quantum) . . . we always did the fishing.

BOB: But we fished like white men.

JULIE: I have a vague memory of the uncles when they threw nets [along the Columbia River]. They'd take it all to the cannery, and then they'd take it to meetings and pass it along to elders.

BOB: There's a lot of work to be done, spiritually and emotionally. (2003, 2–3)

For Julie and Bob, "fishing like white men" means compliance to a rigid calendar cycle, with a permit in hand and use of modern implements such as gill nets. Cruikshank (1998, 28) wrote that "the continuing importance of things, the visible, material heritage that is steadily vanishing over time—the traps, the snares, the many strategies people use to provide a life based on hunting, fishing and trapping . . . provide concrete examples to point to when . . . teaching younger people about how life should be conducted." With the loss of such material culture and its use comes the loss of spiritual meaning. When considering their memories of fishing and loss, Bob's immediate response was to turn to Cowlitz identity and renewal, speculating that there is "work to be done, spiritually and emotionally." For him, the state control of fishing was a correlative to loss of a Native spirituality.

The question "How do you do Indian?" led many Cowlitz interviewees to express a feeling of historical connectedness to their ancestors. "Doing" of course is inherently active and always in the present. If legitimating Native identity is internal as well as external, then at least part of the conception of Cowlitz people regarding who they are, what they are called, and where they are from lies in a bodily memory and a connection and relationship to their bodies. Activities learned from elders or activities that were taught by others but known to be based on traditional and indigenous systems of subsistence living helped create for the Cowlitz an attachment of one's sense of self as Indian emerging from a connection to the land. This connection to the land leads to a sense of ancestral connection that is spiritual in nature. When this connection is obstructed by legal imposition or disruption of traditional fishing techniques, there is a feeling of loss, of "fishing like white men," not like Cowlitz people.

This sense of loss prompts Bob's poignant assertion that for the Cowlitz there is "work to be done" if they are to remain a people, work that is both "spiritual" and deeply emotional. Julie mentions that she can recall old Cowlitz fishermen using traditional seine nets and spears to bring in the salmon, which prompts Bob to reflect sadly that now Cowlitz people "fish like white men"—that is, they use modern technology that seems less in compliance with effective but simpler means of harvesting seasonal fish runs. Just as objects of material culture point to a means of "right living," so does the land point to a remembered activity, a vision of old men fishing the Columbia River with their traditional nets; it is a remembered activity that is also "right living." Gary Torner (2004, 2), Robin's elder brother, says pointedly: "These and countless other 'Indian things' I learned to do as a child were never described as the 'Indian way to do it'; it was just the right way or a good way or the best way to do it." The human ability to create meaning and reproduce culture, even in situations of social and economic dislocation, creates cultural integrity.

In contrast to Bob and Julie's sense of loss, Gary Torner remembers fishing with his Cowlitz grandfather as a joyful and fundamentally Cowlitz activity, which he continues doing to this day:

> When I was five or so Grandpa and Dad took me hunting for deer and taught me how to stalk, butcher and cook the meat, and how to "Stomp a Crick" (I remember Grandpa saying "that I was probably the best 'Crick Stomper' he ever saw, but I would have to practice lots more on being a bear"). Simply put: we found a shallow section (ten to fifteen feet long) of a small stream and made a tree branch fence at both ends that will stop fish from passing on the downstream end and leave a small opening in the fence in the upstream one, then quietly walking parallel and out of sight of the water upstream to a point which you think you have passed as many fish as you want to catch and then the fun begins. You turn towards the stream and pretend you are a bear, growling and snorting moving directly into the stream, then you stomp downstream making as much noise as you can, laughing is involved, until you get to the upstream fence at which time you complete the fence, trapping the fish in the shallow fenced pond. Then you wade quietly into the pond and wait until a fish swims close enough to your submerged hands to quickly shovel a fish or two on to the bank. If we were lucky, we trapped enough fish for the next morning's meal too. When we left the campsite, we always removed the sticks from the stream and stored them close to the "Bear Pond" for the next time we camped there. (G. Torner 2005, 3)

The Cowlitz I interviewed were by and large willing to exercise civil disobedience against restrictive gaming and fishing laws that made no sense to them, although as Julie and Bob reveal, this is often not an easy option and there is much "work to be done" to reconcile the divisions created between the past and the present. Still, they all find it difficult to accept the world of nature as regulated, restricted, and divided. Much as Julie Cruikshank (1998) would discover that the categories of regulation imposed by land claims held no sway with the Yukon women she interviewed (rather than accept the artificial categories of land ownership imposed upon them, they chose instead to assert their own sets of rules and "traveling stories" across the lines of maps), so too the Torners, my great-grandmother Rose Dupres, and other Cowlitz people simply refuse to comply with rules that do not apply. The rules of the state often do not map to a Cowlitz understanding of rightful inhabitance upon the land. Much as the Yukon elders Cruikshank interviewed refused conceptual categories that confound or discount their lived experience, so too do the Cowlitz continue to thrive in this way on their land.

"My roots grow in Jackpine roots!" exclaimed Yukon elder Kitty Smith to a Canadian commissioner. "I'm born here. I branch here. The government got all this country, how big it is. He don't pay five cents—still he got it all! Nobody kicks me out. No sir!" (Cruikshank 1998, 16). Like Angela Sidney, who understands that her relationship to the land is rightful as any law, many Cowlitz wander deep in the woods and wade in remote ancestral rivers with cumbersome waist-high boots: they remember and imagine who they were and act accordingly. Many of the Cowlitz interviewees learned the ways of their elders and continue these activities in their adult lives. The learning is inextricable from the relational and emotional element that connects all people. Says Cowlitz elder Gary Torner:

> I have always done things the Indian way. Not to say that there is an Indian way so to speak, but when I was a small child my grandmother told me that my spirit animal was the Red-tail Hawk. She taught [me] how to know when berries were ripe and how to prepare them for the magnificent jams we made, and how to bait a hook and land a fish from a boat and clean it and how to prepare the fillet for smoking, and which mushrooms you could eat and which were poisonous. Grandma was my rock. She never gave orders: she would get me out of bed with breakfast smells, or show me how to play the piano by listening to the sound a certain key made, and how to feel the strength of a rope, or let me look into her eyes to see absolute love. (G. Torner 2005, 2)

These connections to the past are specially important to the Cowlitz in a time of tribal renewal. Robin Torner likens the Cowlitz to a person who awakens after a long sleep. "I think our tribe should be listed with those tribes who have been revitalized recently after a long period of relative inaction, bordering on dormancy," he says. "The Cowlitz of [today] are not a recent invention of a new group who never were a tribe; the modern Cowlitz are a group of Indian descendants who have recently become activated to their own tribalness" (R. Torner, 2004). Reactivation to one's "tribalness" is a thread that runs through many Cowlitz narratives. Jerry Bouchard, father to Bob Bouchard and Julie Klein, felt that much of his indigenous knowledge came naturally through a spiritual connection to his ancestral past. He noted:

> Some of these things seem to come natural. I had a song that was driving me crazy. I went to sweat. I had a song I had to sing, a "smelt song." [In my song] I told them to . . . come up the river. Within a week, there was smelt. Did I get them there? I have no idea. Maybe it was some innate knowledge ricocheting around and we never know till we do it. I sang a song and smelt showed up. When our people dipped smelt, there was drumming and dancing and singing and the smelt showed up (they might be there a few days, weeks, months). Then they would stop. (J. Bouchard 1997, 4)

Just as the Yukon elders conceive and describe a relationship between indigenous people and the land that is different from dominant understanding, so too do the Cowlitz describe a relationship to the land that has little to do with land negotiations or passively remaining upon the land. Instead, it has much to do with living and acting upon the land, regardless of title or legal recognition of inhabitance. Justice Rhodes (2003, 2), a young active Cowlitz man, makes a connection between where and how he was raised with his Cowlitz identity: "We were raised, obviously, out on a ranch, you know, in the woods. Didn't have any neighbors, really, and we were raised with horses, motorcycles, you know, fishing, hunting, camping, that whole thing. So we were raised Native."

The meaning of resources for the Cowlitz exists as a more balanced relationship of humans *with* natural resources, a relationship that is often seen as spiritual in content. These resources are used individually to provide subsistence as well as spiritual sustenance. They act as a means of connecting body and spirit to the ancestral land. Living upon the land as did one's ancestors creates spiritual connection. Robin Torner (2004, 4) explains: "God is there to teach us instead in his way of understanding, against convention," while non-Natives and those not in accord with the Spirit of Nature and God "run around madly passing up edible plants and small game as they focus on one species at a time." Says Torner (ibid.): "I prefer a simpler, easier way. I know where all the different animals are, so I just go collect some meat, or mushrooms, or berries, or trout from the woods . . . the way God intended." Dwelling on the land can renew the spirit and reinforce Cowlitz identity as Native people. "My hunting is when I feel most free, and Indian," says Torner. "I've recently taken up making arrowheads and doing a little cedar carving, but it's the hunting and gathering related to those activities that I enjoy most. There's something out in the forest that touches me. It's a love. A peace, an 'everything is now right with the world'" (ibid., 3).

Justice Rhodes (2003, 1) says earnestly that nature is something to which we are all "tied," and that "Natives are tied more than others because of a historically cultural belief in natural religion (animals, trees, wind, sun, earth). . . . Native theology is based on the Spirit and although most of the civilized world believes in the Trinity, they forget about the Spirit part." Other Cowlitz speak of how the wilderness surrounds them, drawing them toward a deeper sense of their ancestral connection and of themselves. Scott Wilson (2007, 1), a Cowlitz man in his late forties, says that "spirituality is key to my maintenance of a close relationship with my Creator. When I am close to Creator, I feel a deep sense of being Cowlitz, of being Native American." Many of the tribal members I interviewed said they used activities in the present to feel connected to their ancestors and the Cowlitz past. Ultimately, these relationships and the conception of a Native self to Native land have shaped the Cowlitz culture and helped to keep it vibrant: what Cowlitz people say and do reinforces their attachment to the land and their commitment to remain upon it as Cowlitz.

1. Factionalism in Indian country might well be a recent historical phenomenon, occurring only in the past century and a half. Studies abound that consider the question of competition and scarcity in poor and economically disadvantaged societies. The forces of assimilation and genocide give rise to fighting and fear that all will be lost (S. Cook 2002, Field 2003, and Grim 1996). Scarcity breeds competition and infighting. It is entirely possible that earlier in time, precontact, conflicts were resolved differently, but there is an important and demonstrable history of conflict and resolution among the Cowlitz for the past century and a half (Fitzpatrick 1986, J. Irwin 1994, and Roe 2003).

2. Ethnohistorian Beckham (2005, 20) writes: "On April 30, 2004, President George Bush signed the legislation approving the CIT Distribution of Judgment Funds Act (P. L. 108–122, 118 Stat. 624). This law finally resolved the longstanding [sic] matter of releasing the Cowlitz judgment fund secured in litigation in Docket 218. The law defined a distribution plan crafted and approved by the tribe." Also see the 108th Congress report submitted by Chairman Richard Pombo, which details the use and distribution of Docket 218 funds ("108th Congress Report House of Representatives 1st Session 108–368—Cowlitz Indian Tribe Distribution of Judgment Funds Act," online at www.congress.gov/cgi-bin/cpquery/T?&report=hr368&dbname=cp108&; accessed on July 23, 2004).

3. The highly controversial Boldt decision refers to Federal Judge George Boldt's February 12, 1974, decision to reaffirm the rights of some federally recognized Washington tribes to fish in usual and accustomed sites, site previously ceded, thus affirming tribal sovereignty.

4. In all fairness, not everyone whom I interviewed understood themselves both as Cowlitz and as a rightful inhabitant of the Cowlitz land. Those subjects who were further removed from tribal activity—because they lived far away, because they rarely went to tribal functions, or because they felt too assimilated—often said that although they "imagined" their Indian identity while doing "traditional" activities, they also didn't feel entitled nor did they feel they inhabited the land or their Cowlitz identity in the same way as those interviewees who are more actively involved with the tribe.

Image Gallery

Author's maternal great-grandmother, Rose Duprey Ragan, center. Siblings, left to right: Celeste, Peter, Marguerite, and Elmer, ca. 1910.

Rose Duprey Ragan with husband, Bill Ragan, ca. 1913.

Rose Duprey Ragan, portrait, Chehalis Studios, ca. 1940.

Author's maternal grandmother, Florence Ragan, with twin sister, Flossie, and brother, Vital, ca. 1919.

Florence Ragan and twin, Flossie Ragan, ca. 1927.

Florence Ragan Robinson with infant daughter, Joann, ca. 1930, and author's paternal great-grandfather.

Rose Dupres Ragan and Florence Ragan Robinson at Pigeon Springs, Alpha Prairie, Washington. ca. 1947.

Author's maternal aunt, Joann Robinson Rogers, and mother, Sharon Robinson Jamtgaard, ca. 1935.

Author's aunt, Joann; grandmother, Florence; and mother, Sharon, at Pigeon Springs, Alpha Prairie, Washington, ca. 1947.

Author with twin sons, Chai and Shea Dupres, 2004.

Author with twin sons, Shea and Chai, and daughter Chelsea, 2007.

CHAPTER 4

The Importance of Leaders and Legends

> Accounts of the past, including oral storytelling, are not just abstract objects of study and their telling is bound up in social, historical and power relations.
>
> JULIE CRUIKSHANK

> In the case of legends, the performer begins with a narrative representation of a given set of events and then reaches out of the story, as it were, to bring the audience into the world that is evoked by the narrative.
>
> CHARLES BRIGGS

LET US CONTINUE THE DISCUSSION OF NARRATIVE PERFORMANCE begun in chapter 3 by looking at three versions of a legend, as related by Cowlitz Chairman John Barnett. Each version of the legend must be examined in its own context. The first was written by Barnett and presented in the Cowlitz newsletter, the *Yooyoolah,* in 1997 (the widely read *Yooyoolah* serves as a principle means by which Cowlitz officials communicate their business and informal notifications). The second version of the legend was told during a discussion I had with Barnett in 2003 at the Cowlitz administrative office in Longview, Washington. The third version of the legend occurs in a report written by George Gibbs, secretary to Territorial Governor Stevens, in 1855 in light of a brief reference the chair will make during a Cowlitz General Council meeting in November 2004, regarding the Chehalis River Treaty of 1855.[1] This is the legend of Isaac Stevens, the territorial governor of Washington State in 1855. In this chapter I analyze both the literary and discursive elements of the legend of Isaac Stevens as written in 1997, as performed in an interview in 2003, and as cited in November 2004.

Through comparing and contrasting these instances, and the context of each legend told, I discuss the priorities that are revealed in each. I recount how Chairman Barnett mentions the story of Isaac Stevens in a most abbreviated form, which suggests that he assumes his audience knows (or should know) the story of the Chehalis River Treaty very well. Next, I explore Barnett's attention to the elements of the George Gibbs report, to see where the two renditions—Gibbs's and Barnett's—coincide or cooperate and to see where they diverge. The differences in the material informs us about the unique terms held by Barnett for reciting a history. He interacts with the documented source and comes to particular conclusions that reveal his priorities, as apart from those revealed in Gibbs's source. This is significant as John Barnett has been the elected Cowlitz leader since 1981. He was most recently reelected in June 2006.[2] Barnett's tenure as leader ensures that decisions made for the tribe were often at his initiative and with his approval. Because he has led the tribe for such a long time, he takes it as his responsibility to know tribal history. Through his interpretation of Gibbs's documented source, Barnett conveys a history in which the Cowlitz prevail and have agency.

The social context in which the stories are told is significant, and so I look at, when necessary, the ethnographic literature that has discussed uses of narrative, specifically uses of legend, to help round out my observations. By identifying the interrelationships of the written event, as reported by Barnett in the "Chairman's Corner" section of the *Yooyoolah*, and the two narrated events and the context of each, we can see how in each specific use of the Isaac Stevens legend, Barnett creates a "category of belonging." In each story told, this "category of belonging" serves to reconcile any tensions created between a documented or Western-style historical discourse and the Cowlitz terms for history that succeed and modify it. Thus are Cowlitz themes of corporate anger (as seen in resistance), familial unity, and persistence reaffirmed by a leader's skilled telling (and retelling) of a legend and his virtuosity at creating a shared cultural meaning by adapting a documented historical event to fit Cowlitz cultural needs from setting to setting.

In his classic article "The Forms of Folklore," folklorist William Bascom talks about the distinctions between legend, myth, and folktale, grouping them all as prose narrative. The category of prose narrative that concerns us here is legend, which by definition is held to be true, "told by the narrator and [occurring] in a world as today. Their main characters are human [and] they are often the counterparts in verbal tradition of written history" (Bascom 1984, 10). As used in the Cowlitz community, the story of Isaac Stevens can and should be considered a legend among the tribe. It is an origin story of endurance, a tale of political struggle and of hard-won eventual victory. The struggle began on a late winter day in 1855 when, in the Cowlitz imagination, the Cowlitz leaders gathered to sign a treaty, the Chehalis River Treaty. This marks the day the Cowlitz chiefs refused the white man and stood their ground, literally.

Folklorist Americo Paredes speaks of folklore as "engaged" because it brings to consciousness "the antagonisms and inequities of everyday life as perceived by the performance community and as played out within the larger society" (quoted in Abrahams 1981, 305). The fact that legends rise in a community is not as interesting as the priorities revealed by those legends themselves, the way they reveal uniquely cultural and specific tribal priorities. The folklorist Roger Abrahams notes that the lore of communities that have experienced social exclusion and economic and political exploitation reflects those experiences. To bring such "protest" material into the open is to make public what has to this point been a private, in-group technique of bonding and boundary making (Abrahams 1981, 305). Folklorist Charles Briggs (1988, 288) writes that the lessons of legend are "seldom stated succinctly and explicitly. The audience is rather asked to take a more active role in the interpretation process. The performance features point the audience in the direction of the speaker's interpretation, but the conclusions are seldom laid out fully in advance." As a listener and young person, however, what guidance am I given for interpreting the story he tells? Is the nature of this guidance substantively different than the guidance given to his larger audience?

STORY 1: WRITING A LEGEND

On February 2, 1997, Ada Deer, assistant secretary of the Interior, signed the Proposed Finding of the Cowlitz Indian Tribe, which was published in the Federal Register on February 27. The finding concluded that the Cowlitz Indian Tribe "meets the requirements for a government to government relationship with the United States" and thus should be considered to have met all seven of the mandatory criteria (Deer 1997). In August 1997, near the end of a six-month-long waiting period for response and comment, the Quinault Tribe extended the comment period another ninety days, delaying the Cowlitz recognition until the end of the year.

This is the context in which the 1997 version of Isaac Stevens's story appeared in the October *Yooyoolah*, on the heels of the latest Quinault interference in Cowlitz federal recognition. The *Yooyoolah* always contains a chairman's address as well as updates from different committees and departments for the tribe. The "Chairman's Corner" is prominently displayed on the cover page, top left. John Barnett uses this forum to summarize the key events of the past six months and to forecast the most pressing issues likely to affect the tribe. As chair, he is empowered to write and have published what he wants to appear in *Yooyoolah*; he can trust that there will be no editorial interference with his content. This makes his "Chairman's Corner" comments all the more indicative of his personal priorities and stylistic choices. Following is a version of the Isaac Stevens story, as it appeared in the 1997 *Yooyoolah*:

> In the winter of 1855, territorial governor Isaac Stevens invited the Indian tribes of southwest Washington to a treaty council at the present site of Cosmopolis, Washington, on the banks of the Chehalis River. It became known as the Chehalis River Treaty Council. Tribal representatives of the Cowlitz, Chinook, Chehalis and Quinault Tribes were present. The treaty Council lasted several days. It became apparent to the Cowlitz, Chinook and Chehalis chiefs and headmen present that their tribes would have to leave their aboriginal homelands and move somewhere up on the Pacific Coast. The Cowlitz, Chehalis, and Chinook refused to sign the treaty be-

ing offered. In a fit of rage, Governor Stevens abruptly abandoned the negotiations and the tribal representatives went home to an uncertain future. Governor Stevens had failed in his mission to secure the aboriginal lands of the tribes. To rectify his failures, he sent envoys to Quinault for treaty negotiations with the Quinault Tribe and the Queleute Tribe who had only been recently discovered. The envoys were able to get these two tribes to sign a treaty at the mouth of the Quinault River that was in the aboriginal land of the Quinault and close to LaPush, Washington, the center of Queleute lands. This treaty was formally signed 1856 in Olympia by Governor Stevens and became known as the Treaty of Olympia. . . . [To] digress for a moment, we all know the uncertain future that our leaders returned to. Whites began moving into the aboriginal lands of the Cowlitz even before homestead laws were enacted by Congress. These homesteaders brought with them many white man diseases that severely decimated our ancestors. It was often said, "Leave the poor souls be, for they will surely fade out of existence in a generation or two." Our ancestors were slowly forced from the aboriginal lands occupied by the Cowlitz since time immemorial. Some left Cowlitz country voluntarily as barbed wire restricted their use of the land. Others who resisted were physically forced from their homes and sometimes were killed if they fought to protect what was historically theirs. Not knowing the ways of the white man, many were bilked out of what they owned in the white man's court. Despite the strong adversity, many stayed and coexisted with the whites. It is an eternal debt of gratitude that we, today, must pay to those who came so close to extinction. Somehow they survived. We can look today with much pride to the Cowlitz pride and dedication that has been passed on to us. This we must never forget.

ANALYSIS

Barnett's "Chairman's Corner" begins with a temporal specificity, "in the winter of 1855," and moves on to name Territorial Governor Stevens. Such formal features as titles and temporal specificity create a recognizable formula for a story by naming a specific time, place, and event. The place, the Chehalis River, is named twice in the first few sentences. This makes the vagary of the phrases "it became known" and "it became apparent" stand out in comparison. The parallel phrases "it became known" and "it became apparent" have clear antecedents: the Chehalis River Treaty marked in place and time the removal of the Cowlitz—quite noticeably, in the narrative, to an unnamed site "up on the Pacific Coast." This may be a result of the treaty proceedings, in which the exact site—what became the Quinault Reservation—had not yet been determined. However, it may be more deliberate—a veiled reference to the remote site of Tahola in western Washington, where the Quinault Reservation was established by the Treaty of Olympia in 1856. The site of the Chehalis River Treaty, held at Cosmopolis, Washington, is not a remote site in Barnett's imagination. The Cowlitz and Chehalis "refusal" to move to a remote site "up on the Pacific Coast" resulted in Governor Stevens's "rage" and effectively ended the treaty proceedings.

What is interesting here is not only Stevens's rage but also the lack of a certain salient detail that later appeared in the legend of Isaac Stevens as told to me in March 2003: specifically that Stevens will tear up a negotiation document presented to him by the Chehalis on behalf of the Cowlitz and other dissenting tribes present at the Chehalis River in 1855. In this first version, Stevens is the penitent who returns to negotiate with the Quinault and Quileute to "rectify" his mistakes at the Chehalis River Treaty Council and correct his sin of anger that resulted in treaty failure. In this telling, Stevens finishes in 1856 what he began in 1855, when the Cowlitz were present: he negotiates a treaty by "rectifying" his personal failure and creating the Treaty of Olympia of 1856. Thus, in this narrative, Barnett establishes that the Cowlitz, having been wronged at the Chehalis River Treaty, are part of the Treaty of Olympia. In doing so, Barnett tacitly sets up a claim that clearly ties Cowlitz to Quinault Reservation lands, as the Quinault were signatories at the Treaty of Olympia.

From this point in the narrative, the chairman shifts his tone. Pathos fills the sentences as the dispossessed Cowlitz went home to an "uncertain future," soon after to be divested of their homeland by settlers. Next, they were decimated by disease. This is a story the Cowlitz audience knows well, and Barnett recounts it. Perhaps he does so to rouse an old anger, an anger that helps to identify the readers as those who have a reason for outrage and therefore "belong": the readers can remember that, as Cowlitz, they have suffered both the decimation of their people and divestment from their land. Pathos rises in the narration, as Barnett claims that—according to its neighbors—the Cowlitz shall soon reach their demise. "Leave the poor souls be, for they will surely fade out of existence in a generation or two," he writes. The story told here involves a summoning by the narrator. Summoned are the competing and complementary voices of Stevens, a formal and famous documented history written by George Gibbs, and the legion of settlers and Cowlitz ancestors long-deceased as well as the voice of Barnett himself.

Barnett notes that those Cowlitz who managed to remain would be kept from their land. The image of "barbed wire," used as a simple but powerful metaphor to denote human-made and injurious boundaries, stands in stark opposition to the strongly evinced feeling that the land from which the Cowlitz were divested was land upon which they had lived and thrived since "time immemorial." "Time immemorial" is mythic time, used here by Barnett to authoritatively demonstrate a primordial attachment to Cowlitz land. This attachment to mythic time is a frequent theme in Barnett's performative vocabulary. Those who "fought to protect their land" were restricted or killed, although it was "historically theirs." Again, Cowlitz themes of symbolic attachment to the land and anger emerge. The Native was "innocent" of the crimes visited upon him, "bilked" or cheated of his rightful inheritance. Here, when we have reached a dark night for the Cowlitz—of near extinction, divestment, and privation—Barnett summons another important theme for the Cowlitz: "despite strong adversity," he notes, the Cowlitz remained on their land and adapted.

The Cowlitz ancestors remained and so do those who have lived to read the "Chairman's Corner." This narrative seems to be a straightforward recounting of the Cowlitz story of the Chehalis River Treaty, but it is not; we are left to wonder at the effects of the Treaty of Olympia. Barnett has provided evidence enough for his audience regarding the Cowlitz's shared ethos of corporate anger, persistence, and endurance as well as their attachment to the land. But why has he not explained more fully the binding effects of the 1856 treaty, the Treaty of Olympia? Let us now turn to the second version of the legend to find out.

STORY 2: RETELLING A LEGEND

In an interview with me at the tribal office in 2003, when asked why there was strife between the Quinault people and the Cowlitz, Chairman Barnett discussed the allottees at the Quinault Reservation. An excerpt of this interview follows:

CD: I'm trying to understand the Quinault incentive—they wanted to displace the other allottees, right?

JB: Well, they didn't particularly figure it was our . . . reservation. They wanted the Quileute off too, and they were signatories on the treaty.

CD: We were also recognized as having rights to the Olympia Treaty, right?

JB: Right. The Olympia Treaty. I forget what the date of signing was. It was brought up in 1855. I don't know, maybe it was three years or a little bit later than that when it was signed.

CD: It all depends on when Governor Stevens was cruising through?

JB: Well, before the Treaty of Olympia, that's kind of an interesting story too. Governor Stevens met with federal aides and things like that and said, "I want to have treaty negotiations with all these tribes who have not been treated with before." That was a mandate he got from the president of the United States at the time. They wanted to displace all the Indians. And that [muffled sound, not clear] but on the Treaty of Olympia, this was the last group of Indians that did not sign the treaty with the United States. And he invited representatives of the Cowlitz, Chinook, Quinault, Hoh, Clatsop, Chehalis—eight of them all together—to treaty negotiations, and the place selected was Cosmopolis, Washington, where I live. And this was about a weeklong negotiation. They brought Indians to those negotiations to try to weasel their land out of them. It became known during this negotiation that the Quinaults were the only tribe that were going to be able to stay in their aboriginal area and the Chinook, Cowlitz, all the other ones were going to be asked to move. These other tribes knew that they were going to be asked to move. As a result, they rebelled.

One interesting thing about it is the Indians had to work through an interpreter, and in order to tell how many Indians they had in their villages, they brought a handful of sticks. And each stick represented maybe ten Indians or something like that. It was their way of telling back in those days, you know, that one stick represents this many Indians. But anyway, it became known that they were all going to have to displace from their aboriginal areas, and so the Chinook and the Cowlitz resisted, said we want a reservation and our own land. Eventually the Chehalis got wind [muffled sound, not clear] issued an executive order not to retreat. But, anyway, Stevens became totally enraged that he didn't get the cooperation he expected. And he tore up one of the chief's papers.

CD: Yeah, I've read or heard that in several different [versions of the story] —it sounds like he had quite a fit.

JB: Let's see, where are we now?

CD: We're at 1981.

I had asked Barnett: "Why is there strife at Quinault?" He told me the legend of Isaac Stevens in response. The 1997 incident had long since been resolved, and the Cowlitz had received their recognition in January 2002, but still there was a residual distrust between the Cowlitz and Quinault Tribes. Evidence of this can be seen as late as 2000, shortly before the Cowlitz were awarded their preliminary federal acknowledgment on February 14. The story told to me privately in an interview at the Cowlitz administrative offices in 2003 is significant for a couple of reasons. First, it is important to know that the Cowlitz chair expresses a frequent desire to help younger people, and he is especially encouraged by those younger people (like me) who demonstrate an active interest in the tribe. He tends to take them under his wing and assign them to committees and generally provide the support and context they need to continue an active participation with the Cowlitz. One of the primary ways a Cowlitz member can stay active is to involve himself or herself on the various committees and commissions that serve the Cowlitz legislative unit, its Tribal Council.

ANALYSIS: COMPARING TWO LEGENDS

In his *Competence in Performance*, Briggs discusses a form of historical discourse emerging in elders' talk as "pedagogical discourse," which is different from other forms of historical discourse held among the elders as competitions or collective recollections. In such competitive discourse, a "little flesh is placed on the bones" of stories to fill them out and make them palatable for initiates (Briggs 1988, 82). When young people, those under the age of thirty, are involved, elders must move from more "general to more specific topics or to explicate the meaning of what is said." They must "transmit" their talk of bygone days "to their descendants"; this is terribly hard work and further complicated by urgency and ignorance. As Briggs (ibid., 82) writes: "The problem is complicated by a real dilemma that confronts the elders in their pedagogical attempts. The difficulty lies in the fact that the young lack a common basis of experience with the elders of bygone days," since a basic goal of the elders is to facilitate the meaning of the past in the present. The elders must "help the young cross this experiential hiatus" by engaging them in the past and the elders' talk of bygone days. Pedagogical discourse can help cross the divide between old and young. The discourse involves collective recollections that occur by drawing on a frame from the past and pointing the way by means of narrative to the now.

Cowlitz elder John Barnett prioritizes the passing on of meaning from the past to the present. Often in interviews he double checks to make sure I have understood what he has said. He is eager to narrow the gap between my understanding and his, and he is always willing to come forth about past events and engage me in a discussion of them. In our interview the chair moves rapidly from past to present, as seen in his quick recitation of histories from allottees at Quinault in the mid-twentieth century to the question and answer that ends the discussion ("Now where were we?" "1981."). As a young listener, I have a responsibility to pay attention to the thrust and contour of the narrative created. The tools, or signs, relayed to me help in discerning the legend's deeper meaning, revealed by a narrative shift in the Barnett's relatively terse and cursory question (and my answer) to his comparatively long and detailed historical recollection of the Chehalis River Treaty.

The version of the legend told to me in 2003 is significant in that it varies considerably in its recitation from the first version. Governor Isaac Stevens, clearly identified here as an arm of the U.S. government, is eager to fulfill the government's missions of removing the last of the Washington Indians from their land and "cheating" them out of their land. While in both stories the government's intention is to cheat the Indians, in the second telling of the legend, Stevens is not a penitent; he is a willing and active agent for the government. He does not negotiate subsequent to the Chehalis River Treaty hoping to right the wrongs of his anger; rather, he is still the same hothead who ripped up Chehalis formal documents in a rage. The omission from the first story of this decisive action by Stevens to the second story's omission of the incident and reduction of the description of the failure to a few words ("they all returned home") seems like a choice on the part of the narrators. Why would Stevens be penitent in the first story and a cool negotiator in the second?

Chairman Barnett, in his version of the story, notes that the Quinault were the only ones to get land where they wanted it, near to their ancestral territories. The Quinault are popularly believed among the Cowlitz to have sold out. While the Cowlitz and Chehalis stuck to their resolve and refused to go to "remote lands," the Quinault very quickly returned to a second negotiation at the Treaty of Olympia (which occurred within a few months, not a year as the chairman speculates). In the second telling, it is not Stevens's envoys who appear as the main actors to negotiate the signing at the Treaty of Olympia in 1856; it is the Quinault who show up at the Treaty of Olympia, most eager to negotiate and hence stay on their land in the remote reaches of western Washington. In his interview with me, the chairman connects the story of Isaac Stevens to the Cowlitz allotments at Quinault, making explicit that strife between the Quinault and the Cowlitz was inflamed by the allottees' relationship to the Quinault government, who felt that allottees had no fair residency there, even though residency had been determined by some sixty allotments given to the Cowlitz decades earlier.

This rightful connection to Quinault is something Barnett mentions in the *Yooyoolah,* which reaches a more diffuse and public audience and functions as a more formal document than my interview might. Late in 1997, when the Quinault had stayed the Cowlitz recognition petition for three months, Barnett wrote a column in the *Yooyoolah* that very subtly but powerfully made claim to the lands at Quinault. Remember, in the *Yooyoolah* version of the story, Stevens went to the Treaty of Olympia to "rectify" his mistakes and create land for all the Native peoples involved in the failed Chehalis River Treaty. Those Cowlitz who stayed on their land suffered greatly for Stevens's wrong. Eventually, through the process of allotment at Quinault and entitlement to Quinault land and resources, they would stay their place but take their claim of Quinault land. They had certainly, in the terms of the story to appear in the "Chairman's Corner," earned it—and this is undoubtedly what Barnett tacitly but clearly wants the readers of *Yooyoolah* to understand. Hence, potential corporate fatigue at the seemingly endless process for federal acknowledgment, and a desire to give up, might be offset by a reminder that the Cowlitz "belong": to each other, to their ancestors, and—as is made subtly clear—on the Federal Register as an entitled, recognized tribe.

The Cowlitz chiefs in the second story are more defiant, more active. They refuse to sign a faulty treaty, as they are cognizant of its shortcomings. They and the Chehalis are powerful enough to enrage the territorial governor, and they did so upon land where Chairman Barnett now resides. This clear sense of history and place was related to me with pride. The Cowlitz who negotiated the failed treaty at Cosmopolis are neither frail nor pitiable "creatures" but instead rebellious and resolute. They will not be removed from their "aboriginal area"; instead, they will "resist." The narrative detail of the counting sticks is also quite interesting, and elsewhere in this chapter I will return to consider this detail more fully.

The differences in the two legends of Isaac Stevens reflect a political and historical savvy in the chairman. In the first, the he would be remiss to assert Cowlitz dominion to a broad public. In 1997 it would be risky to do so, as the Quinault lay poised to challenge the Cowlitz assertion of sovereignty and upset its chances for federal recognition. In 2003, in a more private discussion with me, the chairman values passing on knowledge to younger people, and thus he wanted me to know that the Cowlitz were powerful and savvy and acted with foresight and agency in 1855. In each story Barnett knows which details to add and which to remove to best fit the context of the telling. But always, and in both tales, the persistent narrative themes emerge: of Cowlitz resistance, survival, and endurance on the land. As Briggs (1988) notes, this legend "provides a rich encapsulation" of Barnett's perception of Native American conflict, borne at the hands of the U.S. government and seen in continued conflict with a neighboring tribe, the Quinault.

FINAL CONSIDERATION:
WESTERN HISTORICAL DISCOURSE AND COWLITZ LEGEND

Let us consider a mere mention made in passing by Chairman Barnett at the Cowlitz General Council meeting held on November 4, 2004. While discussing Mount Saint Helens and the Cowlitz Tribe's connection to it, he refers to the disappointing 1981 decision of the Ninth Circuit Court of Appeals regarding Cowlitz hunting and fishing rights. The Cowlitz were awarded rights solely upon the Quinault Reservation, far from their usual and accustomed territory. The Cowlitz people demonstrated foresight in their attempts to protect their natural resources, especially salmon. In 1976, to protect and assure their fishing rights, the Cowlitz joined with the Chinook to "file suit in federal district court in Oregon and Washington" (Roe 2003, 3).

In the case known as the *Wahkiakum Band of Chinook Indians v. Mrs. Allen Bateman*, the "U.S. Court of Appeals for the Ninth Circuit ruled . . . that fishing rights for both tribes were preserved by their affiliation with the Treaty of Olympia," an affiliation previously and significantly upheld in *Halbert v. United States* (ibid., 3). Essentially, much as they secured the right to allotment at Quinault, the Cowlitz were also able to hunt and fish on the Quinault Reservation. This post-treaty affiliation with the Quinault created competition for natural resources on tribal land. Sadly, this competition was among the Natives themselves. The right of the Cowlitz to fish has its roots not merely in the Treaty of Olympia but in the Chehalis River Treaty, which directly preceded the Treaty of Olympia, and in dealings with Territorial Governor Stevens.[3] The story of Governor Stevens and the failed Chehalis River Treaty is often repeated in the context of Cowlitz tribal meetings. Barnett mentioned Stevens during the November 2004 meeting as well, citing Stevens's botched treaty of 1855 as the beginning of a long uphill climb for the tribe.

MAKING SENSE OF A LEGEND:
THE ROLE OF MEMORY IN PERFORMANCE

The history that matters, at least to John Barnett, is the history common people carry within their heads that, through the efforts of performance and the context of community, becomes a shared history bolstering cultural identity. Official history at the beginning is dissension, which firms and creates itself only through dialogue with a consenting community through time. Such history is at first characterized by difference. One must listen to the many voices that gather to tell the stories of the past and form them into understandings of the present. Sociologist Sune Haugbølle (2003, 3) claims that "at the heart of history is a critical discourse that is antithetical to spontaneous memory. Memory, on the other hand, is absolute and highly subjective. However, certain places, things and narratives ... embody a common memory, that is, a memory on which a whole group of individual memories bestow a shared meaning."

These lines of memory are sometimes able to "define the national, ethnic or other social commonalities in a given social group" (ibid., 3). Memory is subjective, so collective memory must also be subjective. The narrated and performed memory of the individual, as evoked and spoken to a group, produces a group of individuals who "remember within the same social framework." According to Haugbølle (ibid.), our present situation will determine what we select to tell about the past. The anthropologist Jon Daehnke (2013, 39) also writes of the "centrality of place and its connection to memory," especially public memory, which is "memory that occurs out in the open." With this framework in mind, let us recount what is known of Territorial Governor Stevens and his secretary, George Gibbs, to see if we can further discern Barnett's means of telling the legend and history for his tribe.

By most documented accounts, Isaac Stevens was born a Massachusetts aristocrat in March 1818, graduating from West Point at twenty-two. In his early twenties, he would serve in the Army Corp of Engineers under General Winfield Scott in Mexico and carry out combat duty in the Mexican War. In 1853, Stevens led a railroad survey from Saint Paul, Minnesota, to the Puget Sound of Washington and soon after was appointed by President Franklin Pierce to serve as the first governor of Washington Territory and superintendent of Indian Affairs from 1853 to 1857. Stevens would later be twice elected as a Democrat to Congress, in 1857 and 1861. During the Civil War, he served as a colonel in the Union Army, was promoted to brigadier general, and died in the Battle of Chantilly in September 1862 at the age of forty-four. Sources are in agreement regarding Stevens's brief but illustrious career, but he receives mixed reviews regarding his tenure as governor

THE IMPORTANCE OF LEADERS AND LEGENDS 95

and superintendent of Indian Affairs from 1853 to1857. In most historical accounts, he is presented mildly, and although there is some mention of his catastrophic dealings with Indians, his story is always told in light of his formative role in Washington state history in particular and U.S. history generally. This story is typically of a "young man in a hurry"—a determined and successful bureaucrat, small and fierce, likened to Napoleon and other notable European leaders.

John Barnett tells the story of Isaac Stevens often and in many guises: at most general tribal council meetings, in casual conversation, and in the tribal newsletter, *Yooyoolah*. Through his iterations Barnett seeks to teach the Cowlitz people a version of history necessary, it seems, as a protective measure against Western-style histories that often subsume tribal alternatives. Today, the third telling of the legend of Isaac Stevens occurs in the most public and communal of settings for the Cowlitz group: the Cowlitz General Council. Here the legend is mentioned only as a brief footnote, perhaps indicating that all present will or ought to understand the underlying and particular elements of the story: it is an origin story of endurance, a tale of political struggle, of hard-won eventual victory.

Remember that the struggle began on a late winter day in 1855 when, as told by Barnett, the Cowlitz had gathered to sign a treaty but did not sign a treaty. The Chehalis River Treaty marks the day the Cowlitz chiefs refused the white man and stood their ground. The three accounts of the Stevens story thus discussed have much in common, although one was told at the Cowlitz tribal office in Longview during a one-on-one interview regarding tribal history, and the others were a more formal address to the entire Cowlitz constituency in the *Yooyoolah* newsletter and to those attending the General Council meeting. In the *Yooyoolah* telling, the Chehalis appear as part of a trio: the Cowlitz, the Chinook, and the Chehalis. In the interview with me in 2003, Barnett mentions the Chehalis most obliquely. They arrive in his narrative near the end, when they issue or perhaps respond to an executive order, and the entire negotiation breaks down.

Notably, in the second account, Barnett proudly relates that the site on which the treaty took place is his present home of Cosmopolis; he does not presume to relay such private information or to reveal his pride in the *Yooyoolah*. His tone maintains a professional detachment in the *Yooyoolah* when he describes Stevens as having "invited" the tribes to a council. This is in opposition to Barnett's first account in which Stevens has less agency and "takes orders" from the president, who has a premeditated plan to "weasel" land out of the Natives by moving them all to a remote, northerly location, thus allowing room for the incoming settlers. Of note in the more formal newsletter version is Barnett's eloquent mention of those ancestors who remained on Cowlitz territory and heroically maintained Cowlitz identity by staying on their land, held since "time immemorial," and holding it against "force." "This we must never forget," says Barnett. "It is an eternal debt of gratitude that we, today, must pay to those who came so close to extinction. Somehow they survived" (Barnett 2002).

The differences in Barnett's two accounts are differences in assessment and interpretation of audience and perceived audience, demonstrating his performance proficiency and a priority for preserving Cowlitz terms of "belonging," given certain political exigencies and personal priorities. In both accounts, the Cowlitz are at the center of the story. In both accounts, they resist a specious treaty with Stevens. In each treatment, Stevens rushes off in a rage, having failed. Given the continuities in the content of Barnett's story, one becomes curious as to what other stories of this treaty exist. Given the chair's abbreviated third mention of the Stevens legend at Cowlitz General Council, we know that Barnett assumes that at least some of his audience shares an understanding of the event. Do his accounts differ from the primary documentation from 1855? These differences are significant, as they further reveal both competing interests and identities in documented historical writing and in Native epistemologies revealed as local legend.

Worth mentioning is the arresting detail Barnett includes in the *Yooyoolah* and in the interview of the sticks tribal leaders brought to the gathering to designate the number of people in their tribes. This hints at the difficulties of translation inherent in the failed Chehalis River Treaty. In an account written two years after that treaty, explorer and artist James Gilchrist Swan (1857, 345) wrote that "interpretation at the treaty council on the Chehalis was a challenge, with several languages and cultural understandings present." Swan (ibid., 345) continued optimistically, saying that despite this difficulty, "their speeches finally resulted in one and the same thing, which was that they felt proud to have the governor talk with them; they liked his proposition to buy their land, but they did not want to go on to the reservation." A translator was present for Stevens and the tribes—several were, as far as can be discerned from Gibbs's primary document—but the translators' facility with Chinook Jargon, the pidgin used, was questionable, as was the adequacy of a trade language to translate the complexities of a treaty agreement and to accommodate the competing cultures, interests, and multiple languages present.

Swan (ibid., 345) wrote that "several of the chiefs spoke, some in Jargon and some in their own tribal language, which would be interpreted into Jargon by one of their people who was conversant with it; so that, what with this diversity of tongues, it was difficult to have the subject properly understood by all." Although Swan notes that eventually all were understood well enough to facilitate the proceedings, no doubt the multiple barriers impaired understanding. The sticks brought by the leaders to indicate their tribal numbers serve as a potent reminder of the delicacy of the proceeding and the profundity of the barriers that had to be crossed to make intentions and ideas known.

SECRETARY GEORGE GIBBS AND THE CHEHALIS TREATY

Let us now consider the role of George Gibbs, the primary interlocutor at the Chehalis River Treaty of 1855. Gibbs's journal entry is available to researchers and often used as a source of historical documentation. It thus serves as an integral part of the wider discussion of a leader and a legend in context. Chairman Barnett has also read Gibbs's account and draws upon it when recounting his own versions of the legend.

A well-educated ethnographer and linguist, Gibbs explored western Washington on the railroad survey commanded by Isaac Stevens in 1853 and 1854 and was later assigned to Stevens as his secretary in 1854. At this time, Stevens served as superintendent of Indian Affairs for Washington Territory concurrent to his governorship. Stevens charged Gibbs with organizing the necessary information to expedite the upcoming treaty negotiations, and the primary documentation of the Chehalis River Treaty exists as Gibbs's careful notes from an arduous week of failed negotiation. While Gibbs was by no means a disinterested party, as he was in employ of the

United States, his documentation cannot be neglected. In it, Gibbs depicts Stevens as putting his best face forward, as a reasonable man dealing with unreasonable circumstances and people. As the courier of President Franklin Pierce's agenda to clear Washington Territory of the Natives, Stevens says he will remunerate the Cowlitz and others for lands already taken by settlers and trappers—a proposal initially met eagerly until the Cowlitz discover that they will be moved to alien territory. Significant differences exist between Gibbs's account and that of the Cowlitz.

In Barnett's renderings of the story, the Cowlitz are said to have been the ones who first understood Stevens's darker purpose: to move all the tribes represented at the treaty up to the remote edge of Washington Territory on what is now the Quinault Reservation. Although the Cowlitz leaders present at the Chehalis River Treaty did indeed eventually refuse to move, the primary document based on Gibbs's notes suggests a more subtle form of refusal than the one expressed in the Cowlitz legend. For instance, in the early days of negotiation, the Cowlitz thought they would be reimbursed for their land, specifically for the land already taken by Europeans (like the employees of Hudson's Bay). The Cowlitz chiefs were quick to ally with the Americans, demonstrating their hope that they might actually be paid for their land and a concurrent awareness of the fierce competition among the fur companies.

From Gibbs's account, Cowlitz Chief Kish-Kok spoke to Stevens: "The French, Hudson's Bay People first came among them against their will and did not use them well. When Mr. Shaw [Benjamin Shaw, Indian agent and translator] came he told them a straight story and they hurried to come along. Mr. Shaw had told them that they would have an Agent to look out for them and a Doctor. When the Bostons [the Americans] came they were glad to see them" (Gibbs 1855, 6). Ow-Hye, another Cowlitz leader, then spoke to Stevens: "Formerly the King Georges [English] came. They only paid them a shirt to go from Cowlitz to Vancouver. The Indians were very much ashamed at their treatment. They just now find out what the land was worth by seeing the French sell to the Whites. Several hundred dollars for a small piece with a house on it. It was not their land, but the Indians' after all" (ibid., 6).

The dialogue between the Cowlitz chiefs and Stevens reveals both a desire to negotiate, and a clever capitalizing on the competition between the Hudson's Bay and other companies whose countries and fur trades were in fierce competition over Washington territories. Long in trade with all the white men, the Cowlitz chiefs witnessed the enmity and competition among them; they have a long history of playing the different companies against the other. The Cowlitz made an appeal by pointing fingers at the Hudson's Bay and other trappers who came into their land and mistreated them. They praise and groom the Americans by describing their offer as a "straight story" and their means of negotiation as fair. Ostensibly, it is the American government who has come to cut a deal, but the Natives seem to understand this in the most pragmatic terms: as a tacit exchange of their land and natural resources for money, an agent, and a doctor. In the first two days of negotiation, Delegate Ow-Hye (later described as a chief in Gibbs's notes) and Chief Kish-Kok also respond favorably to promises of money for their land, an agent, and a doctor for their people.

Stevens's emphasis is initially paternal in tone, but supposedly bent upon the protection of the Indians: from settlers and whisky, to which he attributes Indian demise. From the outset of the treaty negotiations, the Cowlitz demonstrated political shrewdness and an understanding of the white man's ways. Despite the profound difficulties and limitations of translation, they seemed to be trying to position themselves favorably for the deal, while quietly maintaining that they want to remain on their land. Ow-Hye, in particular, does some tricky footwork, allying against the French and asking for his "place" in traditional Cowlitz territory, near to the American settlers in the area, who are his friends and for whom he labors. He also knows "his" land and has a clear understanding regarding its value.

Chairman Barnett tells the tales of men who refused outright to be dispossessed of their land, but Gibbs's testimony suggests that it was the Lower Chehalis, specifically the young chief Tu-Leh-Uk and his followers who actively refused. The Cowlitz, in Gibbs's account, essentially deferred to the refusal, claiming on the last day of the treaty negotiation that it was the Chehalis who had come first to negotiate, and they should be the first to sign the treaty with Stevens, with the Cowlitz signing next. It is true that the Chehalis came first, arriving at least two and likely several days in advance of the Chinook and Cowlitz Tribes. They arrived with the Quinault on Saturday, February 24, and spent two days with Stevens in close contact, while he explained the exigencies of the Chehalis River Treaty.

Although Barnett has read the treaty notes, he does not mention or find significant the fact that the Cowlitz were latecomers in the week-long proceedings, even though the fact they arrived later could well have affected their relationship to and their understanding of the proceedings. Gibbs's testimony suggests that the Cowlitz, in private discussion with the Chehalis leaders, grew to understand more clearly the demand Stevens was making of them, but it is the Chehalis who say strongly on the first day of negotiations, in response to Stevens's request that they sign the treaty: "He [the Chehalis] does not want to sign till he knows where he is going to. He wants to stay in his own country and not be moved elsewhere. All their Chiefs and people have died there and he wants Governor Stevens to give them that land. It would be better even if we should all die there. He wants some of the old places where he has lived long ago and to divide with the whites" (Gibbs 1855, 10).

Again, on the penultimate day of the treaty, the Lower Chehalis Chief says, unequivocally, to Stevens: "He [the Chehalis] wants his own ground. He wants it very much" (ibid., 24). In Barnett's version of the story it was the Cowlitz who resisted, in Gibbs's account the Cowlitz were generally agreeable—at least in word—to the proceedings up to the final day, although they never agreed to locate at Quinault and originally wanted two pieces of land, along the river and at a traditional camas field. In perhaps the most intriguing turn of the treaty, the Cowlitz and four other tribes agreed to relocate at Chehalis. It is significant to note that this agreement was achieved privately, in an "Indians only" negotiation that took place Wednesday evening, February 28, the day before negotiations broke abruptly. It was an agreement cut as an aside to the formal proceedings. While a concession of sorts, it was not a decision that would secure Stevens's favor, although initially he expressed delight at the Natives' seeming malleability.

One interesting point of textual evidence that suggests collusion between the Cowlitz and the Chehalis is Gibbs's aside, midway in the negotiations with the Chehalis and the Cowlitz, whom he described throughout the document as "friends": "It was now evident that difficulty would be found in bringing these bands together," he wrote. "Not only was each very much averse to quitting its own soil, but the jealousy of each other was very apparent" (ibid., 24). Gibbs's choice of the word "jealousy" to indicate a possessive and protective relationship among the Indians is interesting indeed. Clearly, there was a show of solidarity among them. The Cowlitz and four other tribes exhibited a willingness to share land with the Chehalis, yes, but this willingness indicates a move to get land with the prairie. Cowlitz and Chehalis lands bounded each other (and still do) at their Chehalis southern and Cowlitz northernmost boundaries. The Salishan Tsamosan–speaking Chehalis and Cowlitz shared family by marriage and a closely related mutually intelligible language.

At first read of the primary documentation, it seems that the Cowlitz were being tractable, willing to relocate nearer to the Chehalis. It was a significant concession, given that, according to Stevens, the Cowlitz had held to land on "their river" only and desired only to remain there. Yet their willingness to join the Chehalis also demonstrates that they remained averse to moving further north and west to the Quinault, a people with whom they shared neither "face" nor language. Significantly, the Cowlitz requested of Stevens that they might continue to go to their "old grounds," asking for a governmental paper, or injunction, to maintain that right. They also asked that they could travel as they wished. It seems, when reflecting upon Gibbs's transcription of the negotiations, that the prairie-dwelling tribes, including the Chehalis and Cowlitz, created a plan to retain their aboriginal territory on Wednesday night in Stevens's absence. Stevens, at first delighted with what he viewed as concessions, taking them to indicate a willingness to relocate "wherever the Great Father determined," soon came to understand that the Chehalis and other tribes were quite obdurately unwilling to go elsewhere. Each tribe said to Stevens, in turn and as if on cue, that they were all "agreed in their feeling toward the governor and satisfaction at his sentiments but that they do not wish to remove" (ibid., 24).

It bears repeating that the Chehalis had arrived along with Stevens days earlier than the Cowlitz and the Chinook. Gibbs wrote in his report that Stevens spent much of that additional time with the tribal chiefs, including those of the Chehalis, explaining the treaty. The Chehalis had a lead in understanding the negotiations, and at the critical moment when Stevens insists the Natives sign or leave, the Cowlitz say: "The Chehalis were here first, they must sign first. If they sign, we'll sign" (ibid., 21). That is why this refusal seems at first to be a demure deferral, but perhaps it was quite intentional. The Cowlitz had, after all, spent time discussing the matter at length among themselves and with the Chehalis and other tribes. Perhaps they had no intention of signing at all. In Gibbs's account (ibid., 21): "A long desultory explanation ensued. Cowlitz came up . . . and Chinooks. Were willing to sign themselves as soon as the others did, but as the Upper Chehalis had come first, they ought to sign first [and so a] further adjournment was made till afternoon."

In all present-day Cowlitz accounts of these events, it is Indian refusal, specifically that of the Chinook and the Cowlitz, which stopped the treaties. Gibbs's notes indicate that the treaties stopped when Stevens reached an emotional impasse, completely frustrated with the Chehalis Indians' drinking and recalcitrance. Stevens's agenda to gather all the Native peoples in one central reservation far north and west of their usual territories became understood to all present and the treaties fell apart. Although tribal chiefs were willing to settle on four areas, according to Gibbs's account of the proceedings, each of the delegates desired land in his own territory, land that he knew intimately. Furthermore, there was great tribal interest in maintaining berry grounds, fishing sites, and wapato fields and prairie lands. They desired to inhabit different areas seasonally, following migratory patterns for resources as they had for millennia.

Stevens pushed that "each should take a small field and improve it as his own, as the whites did," an indication that his agenda was by no means sensitive to the desires of the Native peoples, despite his posturing of friendship and kindness and his repeated offer of the "Great Father's heart" (Gibbs 1855). American Indian studies professor Alexandra Harmon (2008, 23; and 1998, 202–3) has poignantly observed that that tribal people didn't invent the treaties, nor were the treaties created with a sensitivity to tribal patterns of "government and social relations." Nevertheless, subsequent interpretations of treaties by tribal leaders reveals their understanding of a need to at least partially accommodate a system that views and allocates resources differently.

On the final day of the treaty, Stevens was so frustrated that he ripped up the papers, which named Tu-Leh-Uk, a Lower Chehalis chieftain, as a chief. The tearing of the agreement effectively halted negotiations. In notes from Friday, March 2, the sixth and last day of the gathering, Gibbs (1855, 26) wrote: "Colonel Simmons announced that when the Governor had done talking it was all done." Stevens proceeded to speak to the Native leaders:

> We have now been here a week. I have heard you all. Only one band the Kwinaiutl [Quinault predecessors] have hearts like mine, but the paper is nothing without all sign. The Kwinaiutl alone leave it to the Great Father. There can therefore be no Treaty and I shall not call upon you again to treat, but next summer I shall send Col. Simmons through that country to examine it and when a good place is found I shall say to the Great Father put these people upon it. There will then be no treaty, no promises but you will be in the hands of the Great Father to do as we please. We shall recollect however the willingness of the Kwinaiutl and the good behavior of the Cowlitz, Chinook and Upper Chihalis. In regard to the Lower Chihalis I have a word to say to their Chief Tu-leh-uk. "Tu-leh-uk, come here! Bring your paper!" (Takes his commission and reads it.) "A man who cannot control his people is no chief. You have not prevented your people from drinking. You brought some rum here and your father was drunk here. I reproved you for it at the time, and passed it over, but last night you behaved disrespectfully. You let your people defy me. (They had fired their guns during the night.) You are no longer a chief. (Tears up the paper.) I have only one word. There has been no treaty. I therefore give you no presents but the Kwinaiutl will hereafter receive presents when Mr. Simmons comes to their country. You will all have your potatoes and return home." (Broke up the Council). (Ibid.)

Stevens concedes that, excepting the Lower Chehalis, the Natives had by and large observed "good behavior," although none except the Quinault shared "his heart." This was to say, none but the Quinault were willing to accept the bounds of the reservation chosen for them at the outset of treaty negotiations (on February 26, 1855).

When Chairman Barnett tells the story of Governor Isaac Stevens and the treaty negotiations, in all instances I have heard, he tells it as if the Native knows the failed Chehalis Treaty was a government setup with a predetermined outcome. There is evidence in Gibbs's primary account that the Cowlitz had an idea of being misled, especially after discussing the matter privately with other Indians who preceded them by a few days in the negotiations. Gibbs's transcripts show that the Cowlitz chiefs understood that they were being asked to leave the burial grounds of their ancestors to move somewhere up north, far from their aboriginal land or migratory grounds. In Barnett's narration, the Cowlitz are fully cognizant of being misled, there is little ambiguity, and he does not suggest that the Cowlitz chiefs thought to make compromises by, for example, conceding to move to Chehalis territory.

Perhaps the most telling difference between Barnett's story and Gibbs's transcription is that while the Chehalis Tribe, both Upper and Lower, looms large in Gibbs's account, it is the Cowlitz who stand at the center for Barnett. In every telling, there is little but an oblique mention of the Chehalis, who seem to stand in Gibbs's account as a central agent in the negotiations. Barnett appropriates the Chehalis' more central role and identity for the Cowlitz, and even for himself as teller of the tale. In his telling, the Cowlitz are active agents in their own destiny. Gibbs's transcripts suggest this as well but paints a picture of a people much more subtle in their approach, much quieter in their stubborn unwillingness to leave their land.

Another significant difference is that in Barnett's account (and others), Stevens leaves the treaty absolutely "enraged." There is scant evidence in the original transcript to support this, however, although Gibbs does reserve two of only three exclamation points used in his notes for the interlude in which Stevens calls Chief Tu-Leh-Uk to the fore and tears up his agreement. More modern historical accounts of these events, such as Kent Richards's 1979 book on Stevens, *Young Man in a Hurry*, seem to rest with the final judgment that while the Chehalis River Treaty's failure was a disappointment to Stevens, it was only a minor setback to his grander project of clearing Washington Territory for white settlement. "Although the setback at Chehalis was regretted," Richards (ibid., 209) writes, "Stevens regarded the Indians of the Southwest Washington as relatively unimportant people, who could be brought under treaty at a later time. Michael Simmons did return to conclude treaties with the Quinault and Quileute tribes in July, which Stevens signed in January of 1856, but the Chehalis, Cowlitz and Chinook Indians never signed a formal treaty." According to Richards, the inconclusive treaty was arguably of little concern for Stevens, but its effects loom large in the Cowlitz imagination, where the history of conflict with the white man was sealed that day in 1855. An Indian, not a white man, had refused, had known better despite the inadequate lingua franca of Chinook language, despite the encroachment of settlers into Washington Territory, despite the gold rush, the railroad, fur company politics, Catholicism, disease. Despite all these things, there stood some young Indians who said to Stevens: "We won't be moved."

The story John Barnett tells of Isaac Stevens comes "from stuff I read," he tells me in an interview, meaning that the source of his story is literate and then transliterated and made oral in a compelling turn of events. His story is not merely a tailored narrative genre, although it is intelligently and intentionally presented; rather, it is also a response to the political situation Barnett has endured and brought his people through. His engagement and conversation with the history of the treaty can be likened to literary scholar Kenneth Burke's idea of the parlor. One walks into the parlor only partially informed, but through active listening one begins to discern his place and then actively and competently engages in the conversations at hand. "Buried in this metaphor of the parlor," he writes, "is the idea that effective speakers who want to join the conversation [must] listen to what's happening in order to most effectively choose the 'right' time to come in" (Burke 1941, 111).

John Barnett is standing in the parlor, amid the milieu of official history and dynamic Cowlitz culture; he listens and responds with a very different take on the story of Stevens, a story he carries back to the people with the hopes of teaching them. The scholar Chris Friday (2008, 168) has noted that responses to treaties and treaty provisions often give rise to Native "articulations of what treaties meant to them." Jon Daehnke (2013, 38) has further elaborated on the importance of "unbalanced cultural encounters and colonial control" that elide and subsume rich tribal histories, especially "where efforts to reclaim culture are hindered by a lack of tribal control." In John

Barnett's legend of Governor Stevens, we hear the recurrent Cowlitz themes of persistence against odds, attachment to the land, familial survival, and corporate anger at a government out to swindle an innocent people.

In all of Barnett's performances, the central role belongs to the Cowlitz ancestors. They are portrayed as a people who persisted despite adversity, succeeding against their rivals and against all odds, and overcoming Stevens's poisonous promises. "The variations over time in performances of the Stevens treaties by Indians of the Puget Sound region came about," Friday (2008, 177) writes, "because Indians mobilized the treaties and their understanding of them for the purposes of the day. In doing that, Indians did not 'rewrite' the treaty promises or invent new ones; rather, they elaborated creatively on the original promises and thus honored a tradition of invoking the treaties to achieve a goal they defined."

Epigraphs: Cruikshank 1998; and Briggs 1988.

1. It should be apparent that Secretary George Gibbs's report is yet another version of the story of the failed treaty and is likewise a performance. This does not, of course, mitigate the fact that the document is privileged (its placement, its frequent reference by readers, its prevalence in citation, etc.) as an authoritative source and given credibility as such. I definitely consider it a narrative performance.
2. John Barnett died on June 15, 2008, and was succeeded by Tribal Vice Chair William Iyall.
3. The Treaty of Olympia in 1855 and 1856 created the original ten thousand acres for the Quinault Reservation and was negotiated, after the failed Chehalis River Treaty of 1855, with the Quinault and Quileute Tribes, excluding those who had angered Stevens in early 1855 (i.e., the Chehalis, Cowlitz, and others).

CHAPTER 5

The Importance of Personal History Narrative

PERSONAL HISTORY NARRATIVE, AS A GENRE OF PERFORMANCE, can tell us about the priorities of the teller and involve us in his or her dynamic experience. The relationship between teller and listener is deepened by the acts of telling and hearing, creating an experiential connection between teller and listener. This exchange can strengthen relationships and build an experience in common, one that can be drawn upon later. All life history narrative is inherently performative, for it has a social function; it is not a set of discrete "meanings embedded within texts and waiting to be discovered [for] meaning is not fixed, it must be studied in practice, in the small interactions of everyday life" (Cruikshank 1995, 70).

Folklorist Cristina Sanchez-Carretero (1999, 17), in her study of oral history, life story, and personal history narrative, comes to the conclusion that "life story and personal history narrative are terms that have been used more or less consistently," but that oral histories tend to be fraught with competing interpretations and applications of the term. While oral historians refer to "oral history as a technique" of the trade, oral history has also been viewed as a "product" in anthropology, a means by which the anthropologist can comb the oral historical texts for other, more salient cultural information. More recently, however, in both folklore and anthropology, the ethnographer has turned to considering the content of oral history as a document in and of itself. Regarding biography, Sanchez-Carretero (ibid., 9) claims the differences between biography, "a text written by a biographer about the subject," and oral history lay in their truth claims, wherein an oral history is always assumed to be prompted by actual circumstances and stands as verifiable fact. Biography is slightly more problematic than personal history narrative in that it depends upon the biographer's translation of the information gleaned from his or her subject.

The scholar Arnold Krupat (1983, ix) has written that the lines once thought to separate the disciplines of anthropology, history, and literature (those lines being the textual lines separating fact from "interpretation" and object from subject) now function to reveal that "no narrative can be transparent upon reality" and that what constitutes fact is "always a matter of interpretation." Those creating biographies of their Indian subjects will come to understand that they too are woven inextricably into the process and are part of its yield. According to anthropologist Julie Cruikshank, despite its potential pitfalls, biography is relevant in that it "begins conversation between anthropologists" and their hosts, and these dialogues "open the possibility that we may learn something about the process of communication, about how words can be used to construct meaningful accounts of life experience" (Cruikshank 1995, 55).

In a carefully considered argument regarding narrative and its translation, the folklorist Donald Braid (1996, 8) presents the argument for a "performance-centered approach to oral narrative in which text, narrative event and narrated event form an indissoluble unity." He focuses on the listener's experience of the narrative as one possible "point of entry into the larger unity" (ibid., 8). In seeking to understand how the listener makes sense of the story he or she is told, Braid draws upon phenomenology and its emphasis on the temporal and affective processes of a subject. He notes how the listener of a narrative—through the process of active engagement—can inhabit affective states, or "flow," and that this flow exists as part of meaning making that is then incorporated into the lexicon of personal experience (ibid., 8). Cruikshank also speaks to the phenomenon of "flow" between subject and listener and how such flow leads to potential incorporative experience. She notes with some poignancy that even after her friend and respondent Angela Sidney died, her words continue to teach as they "surface unexpectedly . . . just as she undoubtedly hoped they would" (Cruikshank 1995, 55).

ROY WILSON: A COWLITZ TRIBAL SPIRITUAL LEADER'S PERSONAL HISTORY NARRATIVE

This chapter discusses the personal history narrative that Roy Wilson shared with me. Let us consider this narrative in light of other literature on the process of narrative and the use of biography. I spoke to Wilson at length in 1997 at the Cowlitz Longview, Washington, office and interviewed him again at his home in 2003. Informally and in between those times, we would meet at Cowlitz events, such as a family picnic or a blessing ceremony along the Cowlitz River. Here I look at Wilson's biography in terms of documentable historical events (e.g., his birth on the Yakama Reservation) and symbolically, as a means by which he animates and creates his personal history narrative.

Cruikshank writes that she learned about metaphor and the cultural priorities inherent in personal history narrative by "gradually coming to realize" that her interviewee was taking an active role in guiding the conversation and conveying her priorities. "Despite my initial sense that we were moving farther and farther from our shared objective of preparing an orally narrated life history," Cruikshank explains, "I gradually came to realize that Mrs. Sidney was consciously providing me with a kind of cultural scaffolding, the broad framework I needed to learn before I could begin to ask intelligent questions" (Cruikshank 1995, 56). In analyzing my interviews with Roy Wilson, I discovered that I too was being provided with a "cultural scaffolding," a "broad framework" to guide me more deeply into understanding both Wilson's place and mine among the Cowlitz Tribe. Roy Wilson is the Cowlitz Tribe's spiritual elder. He was born in the late 1920s to a German mother and an Indian father. Like John Barnett, he is a tall man. He has fair and ruddy skin, pale brows, light blue eyes, and a warm presence. In interviews he talks fondly of his childhood and seems to remember it very well.

Wilson was born on the Yakama Reservation, in the dry, rolling hills of south-central Washington. His father, a Cowlitz man, married Wilson's young mother when they were both in their teens. "Back in the early part of the century," he says, "because the Cowlitz had not received a reservation, the Yakama invited the Cowlitz to stay at the Yakama Reservation. When my father was born, he became [a Yakama] allottee, and had forty acres given to him. All my dad's life he was always there, at Yakama" (Wilson 1997b, 1). Wilson's mother, a deeply religious white woman, was the one interested in maintaining what she saw as Roy's Native spiritual legacy. He says: "My mother did more to keep me sensitive to my Native culture and heritage than my father did, though she was non-Indian. My father was only politically minded. The tribal council mattered, and land and things that bring money was what interested him. He had no interest in spirituality, whereas Mother spent little time with the politics and money of the tribe, but she was interested in our spiritual ways. I had a mother who always told me though she was Christian and raised in the church, 'keep your eyes on the similarity in our traditions. *It will be powerful for you.*' That's been a key" (ibid., 2).

As he reminisces, Roy smiles and recalls the ways in which his mother and father raised him to be Native: "I grew up in both cultures, with Dad being Indian and Mom being non-Indian. So, for many years, Dad would be on tribal council, I'd be with the other boys. The old elders would teach us boys the old stories and old ways. And that was Saturday; Mom would take me to church on Sunday" (ibid., 2). His German mother, barely seventeen when he was born, pressed "spirit," but his Cowlitz father passed the word, although few Cowlitz words remained. The Native vocabulary Wilson's father employed was a patois of Tsamosan Salish, Sahaptin, French, and English. The "Indian" words rose from his father most often in times of urgency. "Dad would always speak in English, but when he got excited he spoke in Indian," says Roy. "He'd get excited. And he'd say 'Welum! Welum papooses! Welum!' We knew we needed to come at once. Now say he was working on the car, usually he didn't mind me there, but if he did, he'd say 'Klatawa ya,' which meant 'Move away, go play.'" Roy adds, "but if he said, 'Klatawa aaaaaaaaaaaaaaaaaaaa,' that meant 'Get lost,' get out of his sight."

When asked whether he learned any of the language, Roy says with a little sadness in his voice, his animated face becoming still, "I only know pieces." In his childhood at tribal meetings, "the members still spoke the languages. We had many languages [and] in the early days of my life I heard more Indian than English" (ibid.). He leans forward in his chair, aglow in memory: "You knew what they were talking about, but not what they were saying, so you got one of the elders, like Mary Kiona, to talk to you . . . or Joe Peters would be an intermediary." His voice falls away and he pauses, straining to speak, then: "You don't see that anymore [his shoulders shake as he begins to cry, his voice breaking]; th-th-that's all gone. Those was very sacred days, very important days. I didn't know I was on the verge of seeing something go that was sacred and important to the people" (ibid., 2). His usual eloquence and careful grammar disintegrate with his tearful pain. He looks directly at me, and we are silent a good while.

Roy Wilson feels, having lived the loss, that Native language is valuable. It is a significant marker of Cowlitz identity, and the days of the elders were "precious." The vibrancy and vigor of competing languages has been lost to a single, ascendant language. The loss is real, tangible, believes Wilson, and with it has gone a certain degree of Cowlitz identity. Lost is the active language of his people, lost are the people who spoke the language.[1] Linguist Michael Silverstein (2003) has maintained that the evocation of an "old world" language makes a people appear to "perdure," to maintain identity through time. To suggest the languages of the past is to resurrect and connect to the past, to a people who have been rent and torn by the forces of history.

During the interview, Wilson is reduced to a quiet, persistent evocation. In his telling, what remains of the Cowlitz language, and the people who carried it, is pared down to necessity and emotion—like a body in the freezing Pacific, shunting blood to the core. Wilson spends his considerable energy relearning and breathing life into what remains of his sleeping language: sorting the stems and verbs that rest on the pages of anthropologist Franz Boas's protégés who carefully documented Indian languages throughout the early twentieth century.

FROM MANY LANGUAGES TO THE GOOD BOOK

In our discussions, Roy Wilson was emphatic that I understand the "split" he lived during his childhood. He was raised with the words of the elders each Saturday and then went with his mother to a Christian Sunday school. His immersion in Christianity was not only his mother's doing, nor was it unusual at the time.[2] For Wilson, however, the split he felt negotiating the disparate worlds of Christian and Indian spirituality was agonizing.

Today a large majority of Native Americans are Christian. But Wilson, it seems, has spent a lifetime finding a way to reconcile his Christianity and his conception of Native American spirituality. He explains:

> I never was in a sweat lodge the early years of home. I left home young. I skipped second grade.... At the end of my junior year, I graduated with the senior class ahead of me, at sixteen [in an accelerated program]. [The program was a] way some of us could get to college before we enlisted. I was sixteen when I went to the seminary. So many [men] were off in the war they didn't have enough to pastor the college student pastor churches.... At the age of sixteen I took my first pastory. It was a small church, very small. And at that time I was raised in a fundamentalist tradition, and so that's where I began. I found that I kept struggling [and that] there were two different Roys. There was the Christian Roy, the Sunday school Roy, and there was what the tribal elders, the spiritual elders [had taught me], and I was always feeling both sides ... (Wilson 1997b, 4)

As a young man, Wilson leaned more toward his church than his tribe. He will not name the church, calling it only "fundamentalist." He was devout and hardworking. At the tender age of sixteen he had his own parish. But his calling was pulling him in two directions. Roy's speech falls off after mentioning "two different Roys" and how he was "always feeling both sides." He decides not to say whatever he was going to say next; it's an unusual narrative move for this usually forthcoming man. Emotionally, he seems very distant as he remembers this difficult time in his life, when he felt cut in two. We sit silently for a while, and after a moment he continues: "When I discovered common unity, two roads, one road that you could be Christian and you could [also] be Indian, when I discovered that, that's when I found my healing" (ibid., 4). Again, he summons the metaphor of the "split" in his consciousness. For Wilson, there were "two roads," and he felt pulled toward each. He harbored a need for acceptance of himself, and what he perceived as the "Indian" within him, but he also needed to embrace the church.

After a moment, Roy begins to speak again. "By that time, I'd taken a more liberal road. And I learned to recognize the power, the beauty in religion, whether it be Christian, Native American, Islam, Hinduism. In all traditions there are powers" (ibid., 5). He never fully defines what these powers are but suggests that an immersion in Cowlitz ritual and pan-Indian practices helped him to heal and to find a single path. He says: "When I came to puberty, which in the aboriginal tribes was the time to take your first sweat, I didn't do it [and so] these things didn't happen till I left home, as a young teenager going off to seminary, then coming back and talking to tribal elders. And tribal elders resolved the conflicts. In my early twenties I went on my first vision quest, and experienced my first sweat. I began moving that direction. It became a more and more important part of my life" (ibid., 4).

Wilson explains that the tribal elders finally put to rest the war that was going on inside of him, alluding to the healing he received from Native ceremony. He moved from a fundamental attachment to his Christian faith, to a broader interpretation of spirituality, but he is not forthcoming about the process, instead preferring to tell his tale of metamorphoses in broad strokes. Recounting the memories obviously pain him; he alternately pales and flushes and is moved to tears as he talks. At the core of this pain now, he says, is his children's rejection of the tribe, which he views as a rejection of his very self. "The heartbreak for me," Roy continues, "is that all the years my children were growing up I brought them to every tribal meeting. And not one of them goes to tribal meetings today, but what is a real heartbreak for me, the mistake for me, was that I was raised in a very fundamentalist Christian tradition of Christianity, I raised my children that way. They're in ministry and a fundamentalist trend and want nothing to do with Native spirituality. Hopefully they'll find that change, change is growth. Change is painful, but the end result is beautiful, enlightening, empowering" (Wilson 2003, 5).

Roy expresses hope that one day his children and descendents will "get back in touch" with their roots and the Native traditions. He feels remorse that by stressing a fundamentalist faith, he may have led his children away from the path of healing. Indian spirituality matters to him: "It's more important than politics of the tribe" (ibid., 5). Explaining the significance of a tribal spiritual renaissance among the Cowlitz people, especially its younger generation, he says, looking me straight in the eye: "You know, "some [leaders] involved in the tribe are not really aware of what is happening, even though they are the front ones in the tribe.... [T]wenty years ago there were very few who were interested. Today there are many younger ones who are interested in returning to our spiritual roots" (ibid., 8).

The youth of the tribe thus represent survival to Wilson, the survival of his beliefs and by extension the spirituality of the Cowlitz, "our" spiritual roots. Although Roy's own children have rejected his practice as an Indian healer, many tribal youths and others gather to learn and workshop with him. With the absence of his own children, the tribal people become his children; he leads them and fosters their belief by providing prayer, counsel, and spiritual education. This is his priority. "And the older ones," Roy continues, "they're not ready for that [ritual practice] but [each] year I see improvement." He likens the growth of tribal spirituality to a garden: if you plant one ear of corn, many will sprout. When tribal leaders talk to the people about the old traditional ways, Wilson asserts, they plant the desire to grow those ways in the hearts of their people. "If we gain the tradition of finding our tamanawas, our medicine spirits," he explains, "[then] we're much better off spiritually and politically than we were twenty years ago when I was chairman" (ibid., 8).

VISION QUEST: A PERSONAL HISTORY NARRATIVE

Since his epiphany in his twenties, Roy Wilson has been on eight vision quests. His visions summon elders long dead, spirits who help him to resurrect tribal prayers and songs. These visions, he tells me, are powerful "medicine," and he uses them as tools for understanding. "In my lifetime," he says, "I've been on eight vision quests. All different, and all powerful. On the first of the quests the old grandfathers appeared to me, they stood in a circle; there were seven and they said to me, 'Grandson, this ceremony has seven prayers and seven songs,' and these songs were to give to the people.... The thing is, you need to know what to give away and what to keep. Sometimes it has to stay in here [Roy touches his heart] and you have no way [to express it verbally]" (ibid., 7). Silence, and its mystery, is an important part of the tradition Roy carries.

Professor of American studies Gerald Vizenor (1994, 57–58) has written of the inner world of Native spiritual leaders and of their visions: "The shadows of personal visions, for instance, were heard and seen all along, but not in cultural isolation or separation from tribal communities. Those who chose to hear visions [were] aware that their creative encounters with nature were precious and would be sanctioned by the tribe; personal visions could be of service to tribal families. Some personal visions and stories have the power to heal and liberate the spirit, and others are similar encounters with tribal shadows in the stories by contemporary tribal authors. Nicknames, shadow, and shamanic visions are tribal stories that are heard and remembered as survivance." Vizenor's idea of "survivance" is important when considering Roy Wilson, because the nature of what Roy wants to teach his tribal people and others is deeply personal in nature. Whereas Chairman John Barnett uses his version of history and performative skill to teach the tribe, he maintains a distinct emotional distance in all affairs. But Wilson's daily acts of personal identity translate to the tribe as performance and an intimate sort of pedagogical exchange. The spiritual connection of Native practice and ceremony, he feels, is the most potent connection to the "old days, and old ways" (Wilson 1997b, 2). In Roy's view, language, ceremony, and visions have the power to resurrect the past and sustain a tribal core of identity. Professor of religion John Grim (1996, 360) explains it this way: "The inner world of visions is private and difficult to access but intimately related to the Native communities of a visionary."

Sometimes, says Roy, the visions are involuntary, as when he was called from retirement into the Native American Methodist Ministry in 1988. The Methodists, according to ethnohistorian Michael E. Harkin, are a religious group born of the conflict stemming from the Industrial Revolution in England, where Methodism "preached values of self-reliance and especially self-discipline as appropriate to factory work. Indeed, its adherents referred to their entire belief system synecdochically as the 'Discipline.' Submission to the authority of God was the primary duty of the Methodist, however submission to other less but no less real temporal authorities ... was integral to the practice of Methodism. Methodists clearly stressed the iconicity between the two relationships of subordination" (Harkin 1997, 102). According to Harkin, Methodism moved from England to British Columbia, Canada, in the 1860s. The historian Stephen Dow Beckham (2005a, 13) has noted that "Methodism came earlier to Washington State when Dr. John P. Richmond established a Methodist mission near Fort Nisqually on June 3,

1840." Missions were established even earlier in the Northwest by "Methodists who arrived in the Willamette Valley in 1834" (ibid., 13). In Washington State, Methodism had to compete with the missions of the Catholics and Anglicans that were well-rooted in the area; this "emotionally charged" religion had an appeal for Natives, who suffered greatly at the time from the "disease, alcoholism, economic exploitation and cultural dislocation" resulting from white contact (Harkin 1997, 103).[3] He also notes that Methodism's working-class roots meant that it was more democratic in its approach to the potential of Indian laity becoming Native preachers. Native preachers, Harkin writes, were "conferred status among [N]ative people," as they often preached to large groups, gathered up and down the coast (ibid., 103).

In the online magazine *Response*, in an article about the United Methodist Native American Ministries, Reverend Cynthia Abrams (2005) writes that the Methodist Church, eager to amend its history of conflict with Native Americans, adopted the Native American Comprehensive Plan in 1988 at a national Methodist conference. Prior to that, in 1981, the National United Methodist Native American center was created to "address the critical need for Native American Clergy within the United Methodist church," and it has "evolved" such that its mission is to "recruit, train and support Native American persons in ordained and licensed ministries" in order to grow and encourage Native American congregations and be sensitive to their spiritual needs (ibid., 2). The Methodist conference to create a comprehensive plan was undoubtedly the one to which Wilson was invited in 1988. In reference to this conference, he said: "At different times you'll receive visions you didn't ask for. You can go on a vision quest, seeking your Tamanawas, or medicine spirit, that God or the Great Spirit has for you. Other times it happens when you're least expecting it. It's a vision you didn't ask for, but receive" (Wilson 1997b, 4). He proceeded to tell me the story of his early retirement on Camino Island. One morning he was wakened from a deep sleep. The Native American Methodist Church was having a regional meeting in North Carolina and they needed Wilson, on the spur of the moment, to attend. He was told: "Your plane leaves SeaTac [airport] at 8:30 this morning."

So he went, with barely time to throw on his clothes and catch the plane. That afternoon he was in North Carolina, on Cherokee land at an old Methodist mission. Roy experienced a vision there, which he recounted to me:

> I was walking down this sidewalk that joined the building and I noticed on a bench this little, old, old, old, ancient, ancient, ancient man. Those of us who knew Mary Kiona, she was old. She looked like a young chick next to this guy. He looked ancient. He didn't say anything to us, nor we to him. And I thought, "Boy, this is going to be exciting." I figured he was going to be part of the meeting, and I could just see him. One of those elders who sits in the back and never says a word while all hassle over the problems, politics. And at the end of the meeting, he would stand and say a few sentences that would just blow everything away and [he makes a *poof* sound] there was the wisdom. I was really excited to see this wisdom displayed and disappointed to see he wasn't there at the meeting.
>
> [But] every time I went out, I'd see him, sitting there. No one ever talked to him and he never came inside. Every day. He never said anything. I always was in a group, we'd go out to stretch, etc. Well, it came the final day, and we took our last break. The others were staying inside for final good-byes, to collect addresses and what-have-you. It was late October, and the Smokey Mountains stood out against the sky. The Creator lavishly colors those Great Smokeys like I've never seen before, lavishly with his paintbrush. I was standing there, entranced, when I heard something behind me. I turned and looked; it was the old man coming my way. I looked at the mountains.
>
> He touched my shoulder, and said, "My son, do you see the mountains?" I said, "Yes, I see the mountains." He said, "The Creator has placed those mountains here in their majesty. The Creator sent me here my son to tell you to stand tall, stand great and big in His majesty." He said, "Do you see the trees, my son? The Creator wants you to see how tall and straight they are, and to stand tall and straight in His majesty." "My son, do you see the grass all about you?" Now I'd most certainly noticed the grass. That mission must have several acres and I was glad that I wasn't the missionary here and have to mow all that lawn! And the old man said, "My son, do you see the grass?" and I said, "Yes, I see the grass," and he said, "My son, the Creator put the grass here to feed all the animals; the

Creator put you here to feed his people." Now at this time I had retired. And I was living on Camino Island and I was clear I'd retired. His fourth question was, "My son, do you see the river?" I had to turn my back to see the river—we'd call it a creek—they called it a river. I said, "Yes, I see the river." Then he said, "My son, the Creator put that river on the top of a mountain and that river was *willing*..." and I've never heard anyone say 'willing'—I can't even say it the way he said it, he just put such enunciation, such power into that word that it stood out like a flashing light. "That river is *willing* to leave its home high in the mountain and travel far to the valley to bring life to the valley below. And the Creator wants you to be willing to leave your home and take life to other places." I'd just retired. I'd just built my retirement home, built it myself, and had no intention of going anywhere, and I thought "Go where?" Then he said, "What's next, my son?"

And I must've been standing there five to ten seconds—it seemed like an hour—and turned to ask him what he meant. I looked back and he was gone, gone. There was no way the old man had time to get back to the building, and the grounds were wide open, and I was really shook up. I ran back inside to the chief of the Cherokee, and I said, "Who was that little old man who's been sitting in front of the building" and they looked at me as if I were crazy and said, "What little old man?" None of them had seen him, but he was just as real as you sitting here before me. I described him and they said, "We don't have anyone here who looks like him."

I went home. Hours had gone by. I got home and my wife took a look at me and said, "What happened to you? I don't know what it is, but it's something big." Again, I'd retired and I had at that point never been in the United Methodist church. A week later I got a call from the Methodist Church: "Roy would you be *willing*"—and there was that word, *willing*, "to take one of our churches, in the Bremerton area?" What could I do? I left my retirement and went back as a river from my home to the valley below. In the years that have followed, I've been all over the nation; I've been in schools, universities, churches, bringing Native spirituality to people. Letting the river flow to bring them to a sensitivity as to who we are. And that was a vision I did *not* quest for, but came. Such are visions we receive, and I hope more and more that I come to understandings. (Wilson 1997b, 3–4)

A vision unbidden by the receiver. Wilson was bid by the "Creator," called by an Indian spirit, to run down through the valleys to his people. If "the split he felt negotiating the disparate worlds of Christian and Indian spirituality was agonizing," that makes the conversion story here very important in the telling. If Roy has spent a lifetime trying to reconcile his Christianity and his Native spirituality, the story he tells brings together the split he has endured and sews it together like fine bugle beads, to create a colorful design. It is a design of Roy's making, yet not of his asking. At the heart of his story is the call to right action and service. There is something bigger than our human understanding, and it is benign and has a vision for us that somehow corresponds to our own.

Why was it that Roy Wilson wanted to tell this particular story about himself, on this particular day, when we met to discuss his legacy and status as an elder in the Cowlitz Tribe? What was the prize, the pivot, the item of greatest importance for him, in the telling? It is clear in all Wilson says that he feels guided and controlled by a force larger than himself. When he speaks of his faith, he makes multiple references to God, calling him the "Great Spirit," or "Creator," or "God," alternately and interchangeably. He has summoned visions and gone on quests for many years to affirm his belief in God and Creator. The story of the old man and the mission holds proof for Wilson of something essential: that there is not only a Christian God, which Wilson does not doubt, but proof that this is a God who unites both the white man's Christian faith and Native spirituality. Roy's vision was of an ancient, ancient man, a Native inhabiting his aboriginal land.

The story elicits an important, decisive moment for Wilson. He had spent most of his life trying to figure out how to unite the red and the white, Native and Christian beliefs. Although he had visions, and things happened to him, and while he quested and studied, all activities that helped him to synthesize his Christian faith and his spiritual teaching from Cowlitz elders, still he had not yet had a demonstration from God himself. Finally, here at the mission came a vision unbidden. It was the burning bush, the clear voice of God, articulated and transmuted through the vision of an ancient

Native man. Wilson did not summon his vision; he did not even want or expect to travel to the mission. He had been asked early that very morning, the day of the event; he was practically dragged into it—then, "boom." Out of the blue, completely out of his control, came proof of that which he had only suspected: that the two faiths, Native and non-Native, were meant to unite. That he was the vessel of God and also of the Creator, meant to carry a message as natural and without artifice as the river, a message as guileless as the grass and the mountain.

What Wilson saw and heard that day was compelling. So compelling he was unable to refuse it, although he had never set foot as a minister in a Methodist church. His retirement home was built and waiting for him. He had done his share. But he came back, in his late fifties, to a profession he had left in his twenties, back to a life of Christian religion that had previously demanded breaks in continuity and character. Rather than discuss his faith in terms of breaks and bifurcation, Roy now likens himself to a river, speaking in terms of "flow."

Harkin (1997, 103) has described the "dialogic relationship between the Heiltsuks [Natives] and the Methodist missionaries as referring to the emotions of the soul," writing that we must mind the etymology of the word "evangelical," which in its noun form means "'good news' in ecclesiastical Greek. . . . Evangelism is above all a type of centered discourse; it involves the broadcasting of good news from a central space." This seems to be how Roy conceives of his ministry. When I asked how his ministry is currently received, he said:

> I speak in Methodist churches, Baptist, Presbyterian churches, Catholic churches. But being Methodist, I've spent more time in the Methodist church than any, the pulpits of 146 of some 230 churches . . . and I challenge them with the need for Native American spirituality. Often people are coming because they want to learn medicine powers at medicine seminars. If they are *not* coming to hear what I say, I find that the people are not indifferent to what I say, they're divided. They either come up afterward aglow and say, "What a breath of fresh air you are," or "Roy, I've believed these things all my life but the church has never said it." They love me or hate me; sometimes I'm a demon straight out of hell. You've got to

accept all that and know that that's what happens when you're on the . . . cutting edge and bringing information. (Wilson 1997b, 11)

It is interesting to see how Wilson conceives of himself at the dividing line, the "cutting edge" (ibid., 11). By his admission, he is either hated or loved, a demon from hell, or the courier of vital information. This metaphor of division (forks in the road, being pulled apart, two selves, two lives) consistently appears when he discusses his faith(s), although it seems significant that it is he, through his "eclectical" faith, who is doing the cutting. He suffers the division no more. The nature of Roy's own cut is difficult for him to articulate, but it is apparent that the cut is mended by bringing Indian faith to Methodist and Christian outsiders. In his estimation, this complements his commensurate need to bring Indian faith to the Cowlitz themselves.

Roy's function as a spiritual elder and leader in the tribe cannot be underestimated. All who attend tribal meetings, and they are many, know him by sight and most know him by name, for I have witnessed the warm greetings and exchanges on numerous occasions. Still others with whom I have spoken study with Roy in private spiritual practice at his home, and many read his books enthusiastically, especially the mythologies. Wilson sees Native American spirituality as an antidote to the excesses of Christianity, especially fundamentalism, which makes divisions between people and faith. This disturbs him. He explains:

> What is important is that we do not allow ourselves in reformation or revolution of this kind [to] become so fundamentalist that we fence others out and thus fence ourselves in. It is important we're eclectical and we author our own cultural understanding, with honor and respect for everyone no matter who they are. All people have experiences and if we all come together in the sacred hoop, I don't care who they are and where they come from, [we must form a] sacred circle of life together with honor and respect for each other. As long as I have that, I can meet with anyone, no matter what, even if they're diametrically opposed to me. I don't defy them; I just suggest some things they might consider. And I listen to them. I have learned some really beautiful things. (Wilson 1997b, 11)

This elusive "eclectical" proves to be Roy Wilson's éclat; he is on the road around the United States and around the world, serving the vision he has for his tribal people.

1. Cowlitz language restoration was something that I took on for the Cowlitz Tribe at the behest of our tribal chair in 2003 and 2004. In 2004, I wrote, and the Cowlitz Tribe received, a preliminary language preservation grant designed to help us assess the state of our language. The Administration for Native Americans (ANA) is a division of the U.S. Department of Health and Human Services, located within the Administration for Children and Families. The ANA offers a series of grants and funding designed to help research, develop, and preserve Native languages. Having secured the grant, I and members of the Cowlitz Cultural Committee conducted the research and ensured that we met grant measures.

    Throughout 2003 and 2004, I also traveled to the Chehalis Reservation, where I studied with Marla Dupuis, then the director of Chehalis language outreach, and Dr. Dale Kinkade, a linguist from British Columbia. In cooperation with members of the Chehalis Tribe, we studied both the pronunciation of the language and some translations of it. I also studied the Lower Cowlitz language with Kinkade. During my studies I sought certification with the state of Washington to be a teacher of culture and language, and I was likewise involved in language preservation workshops and other efforts throughout 2003 and 2004. The ANA funding allowed for consultation with Kinkade, whose final work was producing the *Cowlitz Dictionary and Grammatical Sketch*, published posthumously through the University of Montana Press in 2004. The tribe has not yet sought a second ANA grant because results were inconclusive as to what language remained and because resources to follow up on leads were scarce. Sadly, though results suggested that there might be living speakers on the Warm Springs and Yakama Reservations, I left the employ of the tribe, and efforts to continue language research appear to have diminished.

    Cowlitz tribal member Michael Hubbs has personally taken on the role of revitalizing the Lower Cowlitz language. To teach language classes, Hubbs uses the *Cowlitz Dictionary* and follows pronunciation as it has been recorded by Kinkade. He is also indexing fifty-four recordings Kinkade made of the Maspalie sisters in the 1970s and converting them to a usable digital format.

2. Chief among the social institutions at the time of the Trail of Tears were the Christian church parishes. According to the scholar Joan Weibel-Orlando (1991, 87), "Proselytization... had begun in the last decade of the eighteenth century. By the first two decades of the nineteenth century, Baptist, Presbyterian, and Methodist missionaries, especially, had insinuated themselves in significant ways." By the nineteenth century in Cowlitz territory, along the Cowlitz River and to the Cowlitz Prairie came Fathers Blanchet and Demers. In 1838 they made the "harrowing journey from the Red River [Canada] to the Columbia" to establish Catholic missions along the Cowlitz River (Blanchet 1956, 3).

3. In *The Shaker Religion of the Northwest* (1949), folklorist and anthropologist Erna Gunther traces the diffusion of the Shaker faith from its beginnings on Squaxin

Island in Washington's southern Puget Sound through a rapid fifty-year spread as far south as California and east to "a midpoint on the east coast of Vancouver Island" (Gunther 1949, 42). Scholar Leo Heaney (1984) notes, citing Homer Barnett (1972) and Frank Mooney (1893), that the Shaker religion would have limited appeal for the Cowlitz, save for those who had close relatives at Chehalis and Yakama. Few Cowlitz today practice the Shaker faith.

CHAPTER 6

The Importance of Personal History Narrative in Shaping Oral History and Myth

> Each sphere of life has, as it were, produced its own tribe
> of storytellers. Each of these tribes preserves some of its
> characteristics centuries later.
>
> WALTER BENJAMIN

> [It] is not so much a question of different sorts of community
> members, but of the multiple interactive worlds of individuals.
>
> DOROTHY NOYES

THIS CHAPTER LOOKS AT COWLITZ SPIRITUAL LEADER ROY WILSON and the significance of the social context of the Cowlitz General Council. A more detailed consideration of his performance in that context illuminates the priorities that emerge in his personal history narrative. Wilson's recurrent themes of cultural preservation through memory and persistence against the odds materialize during General Council meetings and demonstrate continuity between Wilson's personal history narrative (told to me privately in 1997) and his performance of oral history and recorded myth (publicly communicated in 2004). This continuity extends to the wider group of the Cowlitz Tribe, and Wilson's conception and performance of his Cowlitz identity serves ultimately to reinforce Cowlitz collective identity. His identity is meaningful to him and to the tribe as a whole, as it is actively negotiated within the group. Wilson uses myth (as well as legend) to inform collective identity. The "Myth of Little Horse" (originally "The Horse Race"), told later in this chapter, functions for the wider group as a "categor[y] of belonging," as Julie Cruikshank (1998) has called it.

Roy Wilson struggles in the telling of this myth to connect future and past, text and context, thus smoothing over potential historical discursive ruptures that threaten group cohesiveness, such as the implications of language loss for cultural survival. Despite this, however, such narrative can also engage the listener as an active participant by means of his or her own experiential engagement with its telling. As the listener tracks the narrative life events relayed, he or she also simultaneously makes sense of their arrangement. In doing so, the listener comes to realize the narrated intent (Braid 1996). Although the scholar Donald Braid (ibid., 20) has used this critical idea to explain the dynamic and performative role of the narrator to one's own life and narrative, he leaves room for further interpretation by suggesting that narratives can be "thought with," claiming that narrative, as an experiential resource, "is not static" and can be "taken apart" and "thought about" and, in the case of the listener, "thought with and thought through in an attempt to understand." Braid (ibid., 8) claims that every narrative "combines two dimensions in various proportions, one chronological and the other non-chronological." It is the nonchronological element, the "configurational dimension," by which we may create "significant wholes out of scattered events" (ibid., 8). "Following a narrative is not a linear process," Braid (ibid., 9) says, and meaning is thus generated by the very act of following, filling in the gaps between past and present and attempting to make the whole cohere.

ETHNOSEMANTIC DISPLAYS OF IDENTITY AND THE IMPORTANCE OF THE WORD "KLAHOWYA"

The time has arrived, during the Cowlitz General Council meeting, for the spiritual address. The elders, who neatly populate the first few rows, seem to brighten as they wait for Roy Wilson's approach. Their eyes focus up front, on the tribal council members seated at a long table and facing the crowd. The elders wave, nod, and smile to passersby and to the council members, most of whom are related to them. From the back, a resonant voice makes its way around the aisles. The energetic chatter of the crowd, some three hundred people this day, settles to quiet murmurs and then, finally, to silence, as Cowlitz Spiritual Elder Wilson walks to the front, setting the stage for his address. His long hair is braided today, and he wears a ceremonial ribbon shirt of bright blue cloth and pink ribbons. Though his size (tall) and dress (ceremonial) denote his station, Wilson's countenance is not intimidating. He tells the crowd he is "honored" to be before them, and today is an especially important day: it marks the distribution of funds, known as Docket 218, from the U.S. government to the tribe.

Many of the Cowlitz people have waited for decades for these funds, since the early 1970s, when they gathered after the final decision of the Indian Claims Commission (ICC) for a series of meetings and tribal negotiation. My own grandmother Florence attended those meetings faithfully, telling my mother Sharon: "One day we will have back what we lost." Today, at this General Council meeting on November 6, 2004, the Docket 218 distribution is formally announced by Cowlitz Tribal Chairman John Barnett. Despite the air of excitement, it is also a somber day, for there are many Cowlitz who died before they saw the culmination of this particular tribal effort.

Roy Wilson has been involved in tribal politics since his young adulthood. He has also been interested in the charismatic tradition of his German mother. Engaged in the spiritual traditions of his people, a lover of language, an amateur historian, how would it come to be that Roy would articulate his leadership in the tribe? His interest, as he has expressed it to me, lay in the protection of a people whose unity has been threatened by outside forces (i.e., the policies of the U.S. government and the Cowlitz's land loss). Under these circumstances, what might be an acceptable means of relaying his priorities for the Cowlitz, seen through his own life history as themes of active preservation against cultural loss and faith in a continuation of Cowlitz culture and people? For Wilson, identity making within his tribe poses a triple threat, as he has historically felt drawn to and compromised by fundamental Christian beliefs, which he sees as hostile to Native belief systems. He has also felt compelled, being no stranger to the federal political process, to adhere to certain standards of "Indianness" established from outside his tribe.

Wilson begins his address to the Cowlitz people. "Klahowya," he says to them. The word *klahowya* comes from the Chinook Jargon *klahawyem*. It is borrowed and widely used by the Cowlitz as a salutation meaning both "hello" and "good-bye." Its earlier connotations, meaning "humble" and "poor," have long been out of currency, but the gusto of the word wears well as an exuberant "hello." *Klahowya* is also a Native greeting that the Cowlitz as a group recognize and reciprocate as a marker of their Cowlitz identity; they respond with a hearty *klahowya* back to Roy. In his article on ethnolinguistic recognition the scholar Michael Silverstein (2003) considers the importance of shared, specific language use among the Wasco Wishram people, which gives rise to scheduling of emblematic identity displays. Through these displays a minority speaker deliberately evokes his language as a claim in space and time to a particular identity. Silverstein (ibid., 539) explains:

> Sometimes, a speaker uses special linguistic expressions of a particular language as identity markers... performing thus a little embedded ritual act of emblematic identity marking, and, for the addressees in the in-group, summoning all the pregnant cultural meanings called up by use of the special term. Even while speaking local English, Wasco and Wishram heritage people on the Warm Springs or Yakama Reservations in Oregon and Washington states, respectively, will say of some young man that he is "*Sk'uly*-ing" around... using the Kiksht (Wasco-Wishram) word, *Sk'úlia*, for the myth actor Coyote, the trickster-transformer of the age before people. (Sahaptin-language heritage folks will use the corresponding denominative verb "*Spilyay*-ing.") The local anchoring of such ritual acts of ethnolinguistic identity in these reservation communities... performs, respectively, Wasco and Sahaptin identity.

So too, with a simple "hello" or "klahowya," Wilson establishes a shared identity among the Cowlitz people. The audience is aware that the time to listen to their elder, the time for prayer and reflection, is marked and so begun. Because use of such terms invokes special, shared cultural knowledge on each occasion of use, the terms present those in the communicative act with the opportunity of acknowledgment by a response that recognizes this fact. Such acts of usage can be groupness-affirming acts of rich, comfortable, and private meanings of belonging, of being in the performed center of a group.

THE IMPORTANCE OF REMEMBERING AN ELDER: COWLITZ MARY KIONA AND ORAL HISTORY

Wilson always centers his invocation on important spiritual lessons, ones he believes will ground and educate his people. Today, because he will be blessing photographs of her, gifted to the tribe by an active member, he begins with a talk about Mary Kiona. She was (and still is) a revered Cowlitz elder, a grandmother to the tribe. She died in 1970, when she was well over one hundred years old. "Mary Kiona celebrated her 100th birthday in 1949," says Roy. "Were any of you here?"

Roy knows in asking the question that *he* was there to celebrate, a young and impressionable man, among the polyglot group that buzzed with excitement on that special day. He frequently summons the memories of his childhood, "precious days," in which the Cowlitz people gathered and the adults interpreted for the children the languages heard at a meeting. Snippets of spare Chinook Jargon, loads of Sahaptin Upper Cowlitz, a trace of Tsamosan Salish, perhaps. Roy Wilson was there, and he evokes the resonances of time for the audience present in today's meeting. Temporal proximity to a past vastly changed is a theme Wilson presents to the Cowlitz people with great frequency. When asked whether they too attended Mary Kiona's centenary celebration, no one raises his or her hand, although a few elders sitting up front fidget and look as if they should like to raise their hands. Out of respect, it seems, or perhaps modesty, they do not. "Born in 1849 in Silvercreek; died in June of 1970!" exclaims Roy. "Mary Kiona was the grand matriarch of our tribe."

Wilson goes on to discuss earlier General Council meetings, those of his boyhood. He remembers Mary Kiona well, and she in turn knew Cowlitz Tyee, or "big man," Cheholtz, who had been born in 1795, before white contact. "Cheholtz," Roy intones, "at age eleven, went down to the mouth of the Columbia, and saw Lewis and Clark, the first white men he had ever seen." In a few sentences, Roy Wilson has managed to conjure a Cowlitz past predating European contact, a past that through his rhetoric is still intact. This grounds the people who sit before him, a crowd of Cowlitz who understand the names of Cheholtz and Kiona, and in the naming understand the evocation of the tenuous thread that holds their group together.

MULTIPLE, INTERACTIVE WORDS

Wilson finishes his remembrance of Cheholtz, the big man "Tyee" who was friends with Mary Kiona, the man who sighted Lewis and Clark in 1806. In doing so, he reminds the audience that there is an unbroken line from a time called "prehistory," an Edenic time whose degree of separation is slight. Wilson lets moments of silence thread through the audience. His face is grave and his eyes downcast as he waits for the story to settle in. Moments later, he lifts his head and raises his voice to begin a funny tale about Mary Kiona, one he has told the Cowlitz people before: the story about how she didn't say much at meetings. How, although she was reputed not to speak English, she could but faked nonspeaking so that when anthropologists visited they would pay her daughters to translate for her and her daughters would make some cash.

"Hee hee, she was a smart one," says Roy, pink-cheeked, evoking the common trope of the Indian putting one over on her ethnologist. Though they have heard the story before about Mary Kiona making a dollar or two off unwitting ethnographers, the crowd is chuckling. If laughter is any indication, the audience enjoys the story and loves to think about how clever Mary was, how she made some money and outsmarted the well-educated but gullible anthropologist or would-be ethnographer. There is a certain amount of pride among the people here, a pride in their tenacity, in their persistence. Wilson grins, enjoying the laughter, and then his mood shifts. The room is attentive but buzzes a bit with snips of conversation and babies' cries.

Wilson pulls his hand close to his heart, and the crowd responds by becoming very quiet. "At the end of a meeting, in those days, when she would stand," says Roy, the drama building, "you could hear a pin drop. She would only speak the Taidnapam dialect of the Sahaptin language." He makes the link to the past, but a past nearby. He uses the technical linguistic term for one of the Cowlitz languages, "Taidnapam"—one of the sizable language families, Sahaptin, of the indigenous languages of North America. With his careful linguistic taxonomies, Wilson reveals an understanding of the importance of linguistic specificity and designations for his people, so they will come to understand themselves in essentialized but politically expedient terms, and for outsiders who judge Cowlitz authenticity by the same terms.

The linguist Michael Silverstein, in his studies of language use, has found that in battles for cultural recognition, such as the one many American tribes have endured, including the Cowlitz, language display becomes important. In courts of law, for instance, Indians are almost forcibly encouraged to use language designations and taxonomies that most non-Natives would see as "Indian." They must provide them as proof of their "Indianness," despite the artificiality of language categories. Thus there is a strong practical incentive for Cowlitz leaders to identify with and bring into use their "Native" language, even if it is no longer or not widely spoken. Writes Silverstein (2003, 538): "Such a vocabulary must be visible and recognizable not only group-internally, but especially also in the larger institutional contexts that license its use." He suggests that linguists should become alert to the times and places in which Native people "schedule" ethnolinguistic displays:

> Occasions of display manifest cultural texts, especially verbally centered ones. It is important to realize that the key identity-relevant attributes of such cultural texts are not necessarily anything like represented "content" as such, but rather all the verbal and nonverbal signs that, displayed by and around the self, in effect wrap social personae, social spaces, moments in social-organizational time, even institutional forms, with "in-group" (versus "out-group," of course) status. Such occasions of display are performative; in and by wearing, singing, saying, eating such-and-such, an identifying quality of person, place, event, etc. comes into being—here and now—in a framework of categorization that is now made relevant to whatever is going on or can go on. All such situation-transformative displays are in effect anchored to an origin point where the display takes place, and they project a kind of radial geometry around the origin point, where the group's we-ness—instantiated in the first-person display—lives.

Hence, when Roy Wilson summons with great specificity the "Sahaptin language" of elder Mary Kiona spoken in the "Taidnapam dialect," he is demonstrating that the Cowlitz "appear to perdure, to exist . . . both to insiders and outsiders, [and] its qualities of difference are understandable . . . in ideologically essentialized terms such as geohistorical provenance, kinship, descent and race" (ibid., 540).

TIGHTLY WOVEN BASKETS: MULTIPLE INTERACTIVE WORLDS

The crowd is still rapt, listening carefully as Roy next talks about Mary Kiona and her legendary baskets. "She wove the most delicate imbricated baskets, the Klickitat baskets," he says. "Among the fine baskets woven in the Pacific Northwest, hers was most beautiful." He makes another link to the past, thus performing the past and summoning it for tribal members. The designation of "Klickitat" to name Mary Kiona's basket design is itself a choice, a strategy that creates intellectual authority in its very specificity. Basketry and its design could change from household to household and village to village, for the dynamic nature of material exchange created patterns in baskets that were and are constantly evolving. Roy reminisces further about how Mary, a tiny woman, would walk the Cowlitz Trail, from the Cowlitz River, over the craggy, difficult White Pass amid the Cascade Mountains, and into Yakama territory. She would walk for mile after winter mile on snowshoes to visit her relatives, carrying her baskets. Visiting relatives is an important and enduring part of Cowlitz culture, and families from Cowlitz and Yakama unite to this day to gather huckleberries in the summer and roots in early spring. Over the past century, relatives who were moved apart would gather during harvest events for salmon, camas root, and various berries. In later times, families would gather to harvest the white man's crops, especially sticky, prickly hops, which were used to make beer.

Wilson tells the audience in detail about his very own Klickitat baskets, and how he has one of Mary's baskets among a collection he keeps: "I have a basket from Mary, it is a sacred memory," he says, his voice cracking; "we held her most . . . we held her in a sacred area of honor." The basket is very important to him, both as a metaphor and personally, for "basket linkages go on and on especially if you know which ancestor made it [and] such a family heirloom is like owning a signed Rembrandt" (R. Torner 2005, 5). For many Cowlitz people, Cowlitz basket weavers are a source of pride, a mnemonic for some of their greatest artistic achievements. On this November day, I sit among the people of the General Council and wonder, what does it mean to touch the beaded marriage cape, the worn berry basket, crafted by our great-grandmothers?

INTERLUDE: GREAT-GRANDMOTHER'S VISION

Donald Braid (1996, 17–18) says that when one follows a narrative, "the narrative performance, complete with the nuances of the performance event, unfolds within the listener's present," and he asks that a listener work carefully to "extract coherent meaning from this performance exactly as they would from any other lived experience." In doing so, the listener will recontextualize the narrative events in "terms of [his or her] own experience" (ibid., 18). Braid assumes a detached relationship between the narrator and the listener, however, saying that "with narrative, performers inform the emergent narrative with a coherence that derives from their own understanding and presentation of the events being narrated" (ibid., 18). Might there be a distinct and perhaps different quality of "following" evoked when listener and narrator are bound in a relationship that is familial, tribal and—as such—often shared and deeply historical? United in a way that a more detached listener might not be, what is the experience of the careful listener who has invested not only her mind but her heart in the narrative? What sort of prompt begins from the mnemonic of a Klikitat basket? What sort of memory is stirred?

I am one of the crowd of Cowlitz listening. In March 2005, I paid a visit to the Portland (Oregon) Art Museum, to see an exhibit called "People of the River." I took my son, and as we entered, we were guided to the maps. Big maps, covering a wall, maps citing broad lines of tribal territory: the Yakama, the Chinook. We walked together, my son and I, to see the encased holdings, materials presented spare in historical and ethnographic description. Among them is a carved bone piece from the Whatcom Museum, dated and cited in Cowlitz aboriginal territory yet not attributed to the tribe. Further along in the exhibit are the Native baskets, the Klickitat baskets, delicately coiled and elaborately designed, bigger than life and encased before us. Designs of the condor, designs of deer, abstracts of reptile and butterfly, startling me, wakening me.

I remember my great-grandmother, Rose, descendant of full bloods, descendant of breeds, born before the turn of the twentieth century. One of the ideas I grapple with here is the problem of history, especially the history of indigenous peoples: What in the past century was forcibly forgotten, what was dismembered? Like so many other American tribes, the Cowlitz experienced unimaginable infringements on their rights and their lives. In my great-grandmother's time, laws were enacted forbidding hunting, fishing, and her Native language. Her peers were sent to boarding schools to learn white ways, and missionaries were quick to do their work as well. Later, as late as the 1930s, tribes such as the Yakama, a neighbor to the Cowlitz, were decimated by disease and poverty. The dismemberment of the 1800s was so effective that at the turn of the century, my great-grandmother—like so many of her peers—disavowed her Indian blood. My Cowlitz great-grandmother was raised with a silencing shame, whether this meant being punished by missionaries for speaking the Salish tongue of her tribe, watching her peers be sent off to boarding schools to the south, where their language and culture were systematically denied and destroyed, or simply living in the poverty that attended her darker skin. My great-grandmother learned that it was to her advantage to deny and erase anything that marked her as "other" in a hostile place and time.

The tribal women I am descended from suffered great oppression and poverty. My great-grandmother wandered the forest to pick bracken and maidenhair fern for florists, pounds and pounds of it, for scant money. It was what she had to do to survive. She brought great sheaths of fern down from the hills. "Stronger than any man," my mother would boast, and it was true: my great-grandmother bore great weight. She picked berries—redcaps, tiny and piquant blackberries, salmonberries and huckleberries. When they ran, she drew smelt from the rivers in great, full nets. When I was a child, my great-grandmother Rose spent hours with me. It is her name, the name of a French Canadian fur trapper, which I took back when I married: Dupree. I would beg her to speak the mongrel French of the fur trapper, and while she taught me her word for love, "amour," she refused to speak Salish, the language of her Cowlitz tribe. About matters of being Cowlitz she was silent. Silenced.

One of my precious possessions is a notebook full of arresting drawings Great-grandma Rose made in her eighties. Her vision is startlingly articulated in her drawings, and I have carefully mounted and preserved them in glass and frame. Visitors to my home often ask about my great-grandmother's pictures, and I welcome a chance to speak about her, though she never spoke of herself. Expertly crafted in crayon, bold and bright, I had not noticed until this moment in the museum that—save for the kittens that playfully populated the pages and pages of drawings—her subjects appeared to be Indian subjects, drawn with lines that mimetically reproduced the same ancient patterns I see on the "Klikitat" baskets this day, wandering among my unnamed ancestors in the Portland Museum of Art: something lost in translation, regained. Every line a memory, and I never knew.

This is the history I have assembled to tell the tale of what happened to the Cowlitz people and to my great-grandmother. My family history involves both a series of erasures and a series of continuities, from my great-grandmother's time to my own. Irony is central to the telling: that I would discover another piece of my great-grandmother through the nameless authors of a Klikitat basket, that I would hear what she had to say in the quiet of a museum where Cowlitz identity is present in the stuff and yet unnamed. I see my face reflected back from this glass case, see the basket I cannot touch, see the hundreds, the thousands of my tribe, reflected behind me. I am Cowlitz. I suppose I have always been. I am finding out what it means to be Indian.

* * *

As Roy Wilson recalls Mary Kiona, so I recall my great-grandmother, Rose. And so it is that memory strings out, long and white, like a strand of bear grass; it binds with cedar to create a moment, a thing, an object shared in common. Some Klikitat baskets are woven so well and some memories woven so tightly that they can hold water and carry it over long stretches of terrain and time.

PRIORITIES OF THE STORYTELLER

In his fine monograph *The Anguish of Snails: Native American Folklore in the West*, the folklorist Barre Toelken urges that the outside listener, privileged to hear Indian myth or story and privileged to see it performed, really listen to the songs and stories the Indians tell. Toelken and a notable host of critics before him summon the observer to formulate good questions about what he sees and hears. Toelken (2003, 113) cautions us not to ask what a myth explains, for a myth embodies more than explains: "Many Natives' stories end with a formula like 'and that's how the bear got a short tail,' leading listeners to assume that such tales are primitive ways of accounting for features of the natural world. But when you ask the storytellers, they don't see the story as an explanation of anything, but rather an enactment of something: a bear is dramatized as lazy, or uncaring, or selfish, or careless; because he fails to act appropriately, he [loses his tail]."

The listener must no more suppose that a story is an explanation for "how things are" than he should believe that the "Three Little Pigs" is a description of porcine behavior. Instead, he or she must focus on what the story dramatizes and embodies. Similarly, Roy Wilson (1998, 13) writes: "When you look at the legends... you will look at each of the animal characteristics within yourself. It will be at this point that these legends will become more than just stories. They will become a guide to the way you live your life." Wilson has been influenced at the knee of elders and by the works of various anthropologists and ethnolinguists; thus his statement resonates with what is commonly believed among scholarly communities, that myth is not a story told out of time nor an artifact to later be stored away. It is part of the "equipment for living" whose lessons one will encounter in daily life (Cruikshank 1990, x).

MYTH MAKING: "THE HORSE RACE"

The time has come, at the General Council meeting, for Roy Wilson to be presented with pictures of Mary Kiona that have been gifted to the tribe. As he accepts the photographs of Mary, he recovers his voice: "Today we see pictures of an old friend." He stands solemnly, showing one of the pictures to the Cowlitz audience. He dabs his eyes, moist with tears. Having accepted the pictures of Mary Kiona, Wilson now delivers his spiritual address. In this context, as the Cowlitz people settle down to listen, Roy begins his version of a story originally called "The Horse Race," which I alternately call the "Myth of the Little Horse" in reference to Wilson's textual interpretation and performance of the extant story that emphasizes the relative vulnerability of the horse and its owner.

The story of "The Horse Race" not only has currency among the Cowlitz people, it is also a story about the nature of ownership versus intellectual property. Roy Wilson says in his 1998 book *Legends of the Cowlitz Indian Tribe* that much of the material gathered is from sources he has collected, which is true. Although in his childhood he heard some of the myths and stories of his Cowlitz elders, the rest he has reconstructed and borrowed from field ethnographers who worked with the Salish- and Sahaptin-speaking peoples, including some Cowlitz, in the late 1920s. In the book, Wilson attributes "The Horse Race" to Mary Eyley, circa 1927. Although we do not have the original story, we do have anthropologist Thelma Adamson's written version of "The Horse Race." Adamson worked with the Cowlitz in the mid-1920s, and this version of the story was included in her 1934 collection of Coast Salish folktales for the American Folklore Society:

> Looo-oong, long ago there lived an old woman and her grandson, a little boy; they were living together. The boy always went hunting and killed chipmunk, rabbits, minks and small game with his bow and arrow. He always brought the game home to his grandmother. She would say to him, "Don't go too far, the dangerous woman might find you, and put you in her basket and eat you." One day, the boy found a little horse, a tiny little horse; he thought it was something to eat and was going to kill it. He drew his bow and shot at it, and he nearly hit it. "It's such a cute little thing, I don't like to kill it," he thought. He drew his bow and shot again. He nearly hit it again. At last the little horse said, "Take me home. You will have good luck if you do." So the boy decided not to kill him. "Ride me," the horse said. The boy got on. His feet nearly touched the ground.
>
> When his grandmother saw him she screamed, "What did you bring home; a dangerous being?" She had never seen a horse before. She had

heard of a man who owned five racehorses, but had never seen them. Now she had an opportunity to learn about horses, and she went far off and packed green grass to feed the horse.

"Now try me," the horse said to the boy one day. "If I run well, you will be able to win a race." The boy got on and rode him around the prairie. "Now whip me," the horse said. The boy rode the horse around the prairie five times. The tiny horse was now sleek and pretty. At first he was unkempt and wooly. "I am ready to race now," he said.

"Grandmother," the boy said. "Go to the man who has the racehorses and tell him we will race him."

"Oh my grandson found a little horse, we are ready to race you," the old woman said to the man.

"Alright, tell him to come tomorrow morning," the man said. He was sure they did not have a horse. The boy and the woman came with the horse the next morning. The boy had nothing to bet but the horse.

"You must have something beside," the man said. "I'll bet my grandmother," the boy said. "Oh, she's too old," the man said. "She's good enough," the boy answered, "she can dig roots, cook and pack things as good as anyone."

Then Coyote said to the man, "Go ahead, let him bet her. If you win, I'll have her for my old woman. She's too old to be a slave, I'll have her for my little woman."

"Alright," the man said. He bet the horse he was running and a slave. He ran his worst horse. The boy won. His grandmother would not have to be a slave. He and his grandmother went home. Oh, the old woman was happy that her grandson did not have to leave her behind! The boy now owned two horses and a slave.

That evening, a man came representing the owner of the horses and said, "He wants you to come tomorrow morning, to race again." "Alright," the boy answered.

This time the boy bet his little horse and the horse he had won the time before. The man bet the horse he was running and a slave. Now they ran, the boy riding his own little horse. The little horse came out ahead, so the boy won the horse and the slave. He went home riding his little horse.

The man who owned the racehorses was a chief. Late that evening, the man came from the chief again and said, "He wants you to race again, tomorrow." "Alright, I'll come," the boy said. He again bet his own little horse and one he had won against a horse and a slave. They ran and he won. He had won three horses and three slaves.

Now the chief had only two horses left. Late that evening, the man came from the chief again and said, "The chief wants you to come again, tomorrow." The next morning the boy went. He won again. Now the chief had only one racehorse left. The boy had won four racehorses and four slaves from him.

Late that evening, a man came from the chief and said, "He's going to run his last horse; come tomorrow morning." Next morning, the boy started out, a slave leading his horse. The chief had a very good horse, but the boy's little horse beat him.

Now all the chief's horses were gone. He said, "I have an only daughter; if you return all my horses, you may have her. You shall be a bigger chief than I. Bring your grandmother and stay with me." The boy came with all the horses and stayed with the chief. (Adamson 1934, 221)

Adamson included a single footnote with this work. She wrote: "Mrs. Iley [sic] said that her father used to tell this story but she did not know where he learned it. It is supposed to be an Indian story" (ibid., 221). Adamson noted that Eyley said the story has a French Canadian flavor and sensibility, marking it as more recent in creation, dated to the point of contact between tribes and French Canadian trappers in the West. This would explain the horse itself as the central vehicle for "The Horse Race." Although the horse arrived relatively late to Cowlitz culture via the eastern tribes (the exchange is widely attributed to the Nez Perce), the horse became a vehicle as important for navigating the Cowlitz prairie as the canoe was for navigating the rivers and the ocean. It is also possible to read "The Horse Race"—a story in which the central female character is at risk of marrying an unknown bettor—as a relatively contemporary reflection of the exchange of both horses and Native women; intermarriage between Native women and fur trappers was quite common and helped to build alliances. At the very least, the story can be interpreted to reflect the origins of the horse and its advantages among a people. It is an obvious interpretation but not unfounded.

We will never know Adamson's exact intentions or Eyley's intentions in telling this precise story in this particular way. Yet though Mary Eyley, the narrator of the "Horse Race," and all other field participants or anyone else who listened to her story are gone, a critical piece of the horse story remains: a people. A people from whom the story originated, who are hungry to reclaim their culture. Although Roy Wilson assents that the myths in his book of Cowlitz legend are by and large taken from "other sources," and we have established that "The Horse Race" as it appears in his book is adapted from Adamson's recording of the story, the critical thing to comprehend is that the story, once estranged and nearly lost to the Cowlitz people (for, as Wilson says, the days in which stories were told and the language circulated were "precious" and now they are gone), has found its way back into contemporary Cowlitz culture as the "The Myth of Little Horse."

A CONSIDERATION OF "THE HORSE RACE," OR "THE MYTH OF LITTLE HORSE"

Wilson interprets Adamson's "The Horse Race" in his book of Cowlitz legends by including a discussion that centers on the letting go of the security of the grandmother and betting it all to win. There are two approaches to reading a myth, according to the folklorist and ethnolinguist Dell Hymes. The first attempts an analysis of the myth by delving into a myth's core, working outward to create a logical "psychosocial" picture of the group from which a myth was created. The second attempts an analysis by working with comparisons in a myth's structure to arrive at culturally specific explanations for how the myth functioned within a given culture. Both approaches to reading the myth seek to find a "motivational core from which the whole might be satisfactorily viewed," and both enjoin a "close read of the verbal action as it develops sentence by sentence in the original text" (Hymes 1981a, 275). Wilson performs both types of analysis: first in his book of Cowlitz legends and next at the Cowlitz General Council meeting in November 2004. This provides an opportunity to discover what happens when a Native genre is returned to a site or sites of potential productivity, interpreted, and then reinserted into the community. In his book of Cowlitz legend and myth, Wilson (1998) devises a psychological explanation of the core of the story to fit his interpretation for the Cowlitz people. Among the Cowlitz group, at General Council, he arrives at "The Myth of Little Horse," creating a culturally appropriate presentation that allows "The Horse Race" to function in context.

Hymes (1981a) notes that myths are subject to a plurality of interpretations by the reader, and although he was thinking specifically about the scholar, in Wilson's case the reader is the Indian himself as interpreter of his own cultural texts. The story of "The Horse Race" is thus reinterpreted and performed, and hence revivified, before the very audience for whom the story in Adamson's version, told by Mary Eyley, was created: an Indian people, specifically, the Cowlitz people. To highlight how such a revivification (through performance) works to shape a sense of Cowlitz identity in its hearers, I consider two interpretations of the myth: first, Wilson's interpretation of the Adamson version, as evidenced from his commentary in *Legends of the Cowlitz Indian Tribe*; then, Wilson's performance of the story in the context of Cowlitz General Council on November 6, 2004. Given that texts are subject to interpretation, and a myth told in context yields far different insights than a myth cold on the page, these comparisons should yield insights into the skill of the interpreter, in this case Roy Wilson. He proves to be a skilled orator by revealing his ability to adapt the myth for his audience.

In his book *The Legends of the Cowlitz Indian Tribe,* Wilson analyzes the myth as a story of cultivating and reaping the benefits of one's personal power. "You may have to bet all your abilities along with your sense of security (grandma), but your little horse can be a winner. You can become a chief!" (Wilson 1998, 320). His full explication reads: "LESSONS: The little boy in the legend is you. Grandma is your sense of security. The little horse can be any one of many little things: an idea, hidden or latent gifts and talents (medicine power not yet aware of and therefore not in use). Your gifts/talents/medicine powers need to be fed and groomed. They will then function better for you in life's race. More so than you can imagine. You may have to bet all your abilities along with your sense of security (grandma) but your little horse can be a winner. You can become chief!" (ibid., 320).

Wilson is accomplished at subtly and persistently asking the Cowlitz who read his books and attend General Council meetings to identify themselves through myth and story, to think to themselves: "This is what and who I can be." He never lectures or bullies, but in this interpretation he is quite deliberate as to what the myth means and how it works. For most of the material he includes in his book, Wilson creates a lesson to follow. In the lesson after "The Horse Race," he suggests that security or attachment to the grandmother is not the goal; instead, security and attachment to the grandmother represent a lack of individuation. Security is negatively marked as feminine, and it subdues or holds back the boy (masculine) from fulfilling his "latent" potential. This undeveloped potential—a medicine power, a talent—is marked by its attachment to the little boy as masculine. Feeding potential (masculinity) and letting go of one's security (feminine) thus means eventual success.

In his preface to *Legends of the Cowlitz Indian Tribe,* Wilson writes: "Your community is the legend and the legend is your community; also, you are the legend and the legend is you" (ibid., 13). From this interpretation, one might expect differentiation to be followed by success. The vision here is one of self-actualization at the expense of the relationship between grandson (masculine) and grandmother (feminine). Given that elsewhere Wilson advocates for interdependence, this particular interpretation feels dissonant or at the very least incomplete. To reconcile this, we now turn to "The Horse Race" in context, with attention to its structure, to see what we might further discern.

"THE MYTH OF LITTLE HORSE" AND COWLITZ GENERAL COUNCIL NOVEMBER 2004

Why did Roy Wilson tell this story this way on this day? Remember that he has said that the boy in the legend could be the winner, the one who invests in his talents and wins big, despite leveraging security. He states: "The little horse can be any one of many little things: an idea hidden or latent gifts and talents (medicine powers not yet aware of and therefore not in use). Your gifts/talents/medicine powers need to be fed and groomed. They will then function better for you in life's race. More so than you could imagine" (ibid., 320). On the surface, the moral of the story seems straightforward enough, as articulated and explained by Roy in his textual interpretation of the myth. But what does it embody, as performed? In the context of all that has transpired this day in General Council, can we safely assume that this myth remains one of personal success through persistence? What does the Cowlitz audience know about this story that is unique to their understanding?

In an analysis of two "seemingly restricted ethnographic approaches," the ethnographer Julie Cruikshank (1995, 25) discusses an elderly Yukon carver and how material culture can illuminate the priorities of oral tradition and the living memory of a people. Mrs. Kitty Smith often carved when her children were young. Her carvings ended up in an area museum, out of context and rather bluntly interpreted as "area folk art," thus eliminating and effectively effacing their content and function. The central question that guides Cruikshank's article is that of how objects prompt memory. While the Western imagination tends to explain articles of culture in terms of "how each object functioned" or "who made it," for the Yukon tribe Cruikshank studied, material objects do not sit idly among the people who use and circulate them. They often function as objects that prompt memory and take on additional meaning through their use. Just as Kitty Smith's carvings provoked meaningful memories and life lessons for her children, so too does Roy Wilson carve out and restructure the story of "The Horse Race" and use it to shape and understand the present day for both himself and those in the Cowlitz audience at General Council. Cruikshank warns that objects must not simply sit in stale interpretation forever encased in a museum. They should instead be described and understood as objects by which people make sense of their lives and history. Wilson has memorized this story to fit the tone, the day, and the event. As Cruikshank says, it is all about the context, which reveals the ability of a story or a carving to "live" in a culture.

Although in Wilson's book he interprets the story to mean that anyone can cultivate a gift and become a winner, at the November General Council the myth takes on the freight of all myth, which is to say that today "The Myth of Little Horse" will embody the history and learning of a people. Today, Wilson displays a high level of rhetorical competency, using artful performances of Cowlitz myth to establish himself in the group, but also, in his role as a storyteller and designated leader, he has a means of telling the group that the myth itself has power and credibility. There is a temptation to let a myth or story rest on first interpretations (Hymes 1981a, 275), to apply a "universal" theory of explanation that is timeworn and popularly approved and move on. This, however, tends to efface the cultural particularity and dynamic nature that can be gleaned from careful listening, interpretation, and reinterpretation of myth. The positioning of the "Little Horse Myth" is significant as its telling comes here on the heels of the historic release of Docket 218. When performing the myth, Wilson takes ownership of it in such a way as to highlight the emergent themes and priorities he holds that day at General Council.

Through his creative performance of myth, he takes the authority vested in him and transfers it to the people he's talking to; he is facilitating their self-identification. He also has years of experience, of trial and error, performing in front of Cowlitz General Councils, and knows what works and gets a response. The Cowlitz general body is mostly a responsive group. It is not unusual for them to stand and boo, hiss, or alternately cheer and holler their disapproval or approval, as I have witnessed from years of General Council attendance. Lesser displays, seen in slumped shoulders, snores, or glazed eyes, are another means by which the watchful member can track interest or disinterest in the meetings. Cowlitz General Council meetings have a long-standing reputation for being rowdy.

Thus Roy Wilson (2004) steps in as a leader to enact Cowlitz language and history through legend, story, prayer, and myth, and in doing so conveys his priorities for the group and, he hopes, creates a moral direction for them. He has a built-in sense of efficacy. He is less reliant on group or listener cues than on his own self-direction, an assurance rising perhaps from ministerial experience and years of speaking before the Cowlitz people. He has led them for decades, and his connection to the community is intimate and strong. Just as the folklorist Charles Briggs says the storyteller or artist must entertain the imaginary sphere of the past, Wilson can be seen to do this by going back and imagining elders' wisdom told through their myths and reinterpreting them for his current audience.

In his classic essay on the storyteller, Walter Benjamin (1969a, 97–98) suggests that "the listener's naive relationship to the storyteller is controlled by his interest in retaining what he is told.... Memory creates the chain of tradition which passes a happening on from generation to generation.... It starts the web which all stories together form in the end." But where the groups Benjamin imagines seem to draw from a continual history and enduring identity that is solid even when threatened, the Cowlitz Indians have to perform a perpetual series of tribal renewals to maintain tribal cohesiveness. In interactions with government and neighbors the Cowlitz people have constantly adapted and are yet adaptive to the pressures of their environment. Cowlitz identity emerges as a serial history that has survived periods of dormancy and discontinuities, hence the defensive position, "We are, we've always been," and the assertion's more humble companion statement "It's all been taken from us, so we're stumbling around learning what it's like to be Indian," as one elder cogently said (Bouchard 1997). Cowlitz identity and history form as a series of negotiations and definitions through time: negotiations with the federal government via the federal acknowledgment process; with Washington State Fish and Wildlife; with hydroelectric companies; and with their neighbors. One important place the potential for identity-making emerges is during meetings. There, Roy Wilson invariably draws from his repertoire to choose a myth he finds appropriate at the time for Cowlitz General Council in an effort to teach and lead the people and provide reinforcement for their sense of group identity and Native "self."

Whereas the role of the storyteller as Benjamin envisions it rises strictly from oral interpretation and presentation, it is more of a mixed bag for Wilson. He draws from myths he has learned directly from elders *and* from myths he has read. His stories and his cultural understanding were only partially received by oral tradition. The rest he has reconstructed from his personal research. He has received his myths by a number of means and through a number of removals and dislocations: man loses the language he hears as a child; man traces the roots of the language to the anthropologists who took stories down in salvage efforts; man memorizes the stories, received secondhand, to teach them to his listening audience as an authenticating measure.

So we should ask again: Why was the story "The Myth of Little Horse" chosen for today's General Council, specifically? First, it is necessary to see the narrative surrounding the victory of the little horse—its rise from vulnerability to victory—as part of the modern-day mythos of the Cowlitz Tribe, a mythos that relies on the idea of prevailing against all odds and persisting over time. Yet this is not merely a story of prevailing and winning. It is a story of love and attachment, told this day within the context of the history of another significant Cowlitz grandmother: Mary Kiona. Wilson tells the story at this General Council with all the elements of the written version intact. In the telling, he remains very close to the text as it appears in his book of *Legends of the Cowlitz Indian Tribe*, but the context determines why the tale is told today and how it resonates for the Cowlitz people in attendance.

Though "The Myth of the Little Horse" involves an outsider chief, the story does not seem to be about an outsider taking a chance on the "little horse." In today's telling, as in the text, there is no demonstrable narrative tension around the question of whether the boy will win with his little horse. As in each textual version, the chief remains anonymous as the bettor until the second round, when his identity is revealed. Even then, his identity as a chief is not revealed to the boy until the third round; the trajectory of victory seems assured and clearly the victory itself is not the main problem or tension in the story. What *is* the tension? The single appearance of Coyote should alert us to the center of this myth, and Wilson lingers over the fact that Coyote has appeared, as he draws out the tale before the Cowlitz audience. Coyote is the trickster, he says, and Coyote is dangerous.

At issue is the possibility that the grandmother might be lost forever. Coyote suggests that he could take the grandma and make her his "little woman." While a funny inversion, the grandmother as little wife is a perversion of the status of grandmother. A grandmother is not a lover, she is not a new wife or a "little woman," and the threat of inversion makes Coyote's suggestion obscene, even threatening. Their marriage would effectively upend the usual status of grandmother and make her into a bride. We are left to wonder whether Coyote might also be chief, since he will "take all" should the boy lose his bet and since it is revealed that the chief is the man behind the bettor. The ambiguity of Coyote's status as the outside chief who could take everything from the boy including his grandmother suggests that he might well be the destroyer of continuity from the past to present.

Herein rests the central tension of the myth. Ultimately this is a myth about the little boy adapting to change but keeping his grandmother (and hence the old ways) intact. The boy must step into manhood to both defy and risk his grandmother, who has raised him and to whom he has always been obedient. He must emerge into manhood (chiefdom) to save her. We see the beginning of the boy's maturation when he first defies his grandmother, who warns of dangerous beings when the boy brings back the little horse. Next, the boy bets his grandmother to Coyote, again defying her and putting her at risk of enslavement. The boy takes the reins from his grandmother and risks the new horse, even though it is strange and seemingly weak, especially at first. In his risk the boy becomes more fully himself and brings greater good to both himself and his grandmother. We should remember that "The Myth of the Little Horse" is told to the Cowlitz people in light of the presentation of Mary Kiona's pictures. Mary was responsible, in part, for helping to repatriate Roy Wilson to the Cowlitz Tribe in the 1970s when he made his conversion from a fundamentalist religion to Methodism and a more "eclectical faith" inclusive of Cowlitz spirituality (Fitzpatrick 1986, 325–26). At first, Roy's relationship to Mary resembled that between an ethnographer and subject, but it grew to be a mutual relationship of deep attachment, and he would ultimately be a pallbearer at her funeral.

During today's General Council, Roy observes, having told the tale, that the grandmother represents structure, continuity with the old ways, and comfort. He also says this in his book of Cowlitz legend. That the boy is willing to sacrifice these things because he believes in something new, and that he prevails, conveys a message of importance to the Cowlitz audience. The little horse wins and brings great abundance, suggesting that the Cowlitz must forge into the present and take risks, while never forgetting their past or letting go their grandmother. "The Myth of the Little Horse" is like the story of the Cowlitz people themselves, who have waited and foregone comfort for many years as they struggled for federal recognition and recompense. At today's meeting, with the culmination of Docket 218, the Cowlitz people demonstrate that, although they gambled during a history of a 140-year engagement with outsiders, today they have won. They, like the little boy in the story, bet on a losing proposition, a very little horse—an Indian tribe dispossessed of its lands, divested of its culture but strong in its people. They, like the little boy, bet something precious: their grandmother (who represents Cowlitz inheritance and identity).

In this context it makes sense that Roy has discussed Mary Kiona, the "matriarch" and grandmother of the tribe, at length this day and then launched into a myth in which the grandmother's potential loss and sacrifice at the hands of the youth is central. The Cowlitz emerge in November 2004 as the victors and chiefs. The victorious little horse, unlikely to succeed by standards imposed from outside, manages to win the race again and again, much as the Cowlitz have won the fight in courts of law for their rightful settlement in land claims and their eventual victory of federal acknowledgment. Modeled in Wilson's performance of a Salish myth, we can see the sort of connection between worlds, real and imaginary, present and past, which he summons to make critical connections for his people as a whole. The years of struggle and lack have necessitated assimilation but not absorption into the dominant culture; grandmother remains, as all who have listened to Roy know: Mary Kiona is much alive in spirit, and in spirit she sits among them.

BIBLIOGRAPHY

Abrahams, Roger D. 1983. *Man of Words in the West Indies*. Baltimore: Johns Hopkins University Press.
———. 1981. "Shouting Match at the Border." In *And Other Neighborly Names: Social Processes and Cultural Image in Texas Folklore*, edited by Richard Bauman and Roger Abrahams, 303–23. Austin: University of Texas Press.
———. 1977. "Toward an Enactment-Centered Theory of Folklore." In *Frontiers of Folklore*, edited by William Bascom, 79–120. Boulder: Westview Press.
———. 1976. "The Complex Relations of Simple Forms." In *Folklore Genres*, edited by Dan Ben-Amos, 213–15. Austin: University of Texas Press.
———. 1972. "The Training of the Man of Words in Talking Sweet." *Language in Society* 1: 1.
———. 1968. "Introductory Remarks to a Rhetorical Theory of Folklore." *Journal of American Folklore* 81: 142–58.
Abrams, Cynthia. 2005. "United Methodist Native-American Ministries." Online at www.gbgm-umc.org/Response/articles/Native_Am_Ministries.html.
Adamson, Thelma. 1926–27. "Unarranged Sources of Chehalis Ethnology." Manuscript in Box 77, Melville Jacobs Collection, University of Washington Libraries, Seattle.
———, ed. 1934. "Folktales of the Coast Salish." In *Memories of the American Folk-lore Society*. New York: American Folklore Society,.
Anderson, Benedict. 1991. *Imagined Communities: Reflections on the Origin and Spread of Nationalism*. New York: Verso.
Appadurai, Arjun. 1996. *Modernity at Large: Cultural Dimensions of Globalization*. Minneapolis: University of Minnesota Press.
———. 1986. *The Social Life of Things: Commodities in Cultural Perspective*. Cambridge: Cambridge University Press.
Axtell, James. 1981. *The European and the Indian: Essays in the Ethnohistory of Colonial North America*. New York: Oxford University Press.
Barnett, Homer. 1955. *Coast Salish of British Columbia*. Eugene: University of Oregon.
Barnett, John. 2003a. Conversation with the author. Longview, Washington.
———. 2003b. Interview with the author.
———. 2002. Conversation with the author.
———. 1999. Conversation with the author.

———. 1997. "Chairman's Corner." *Yooyoolah* (Fall): 1–5.
———. 1989. "Affidavit U.S. Bureau of Indian Affairs, Branch of Acknowledgment and Research." Unpublished.
Bascom, William. 1984. "The Forms of Folklore: Folk Narrative." In *Sacred Narrative*, edited by Alan Dundes, 5–29. Berkeley: UCLA Press.
Basso, Keith H. 1996. *Wisdom Sits in Places: Landscape and Language among the Western Apache*. Albuquerque: University of New Mexico Press.
———. 1990. "Speaking with Names: Language and Landscape among Western Apache." In *Western Apache Language and Culture: Essays in Language and Culture*. Tucson: University of Arizona Press.
———. 1988. "Speaking with Names: Language and Landscape among the Western Apache." *Cultural Anthropology* 3, no. 2: 99–130.
———. 1984. "Stalking with Stories: Names, Places, and Moral Narratives among the W. Apache." In *Play and Story: The Construction and Reconstruction of Self and Society*, edited by Edward M. Bruner, 19–55. 1983 Proceedings of the American Ethnological Society. Washington, D.C.: American Ethnological Series.
———. 1983. "Western Apache Place Name Hierarchies." In *Naming Systems: 1981 Proceedings of the American Ethnological Society*, edited by E. Tooker, 37–46. Washington, D.C.: American Ethnological Society.
———. 1979. *Portraits of the Whiteman: Linguistic Play and Cultural Symbolism among the Western Apache*. Cambridge: Cambridge University Press.
Bauman, Richard. 1977. *Verbal Art as Performance*. Rowley, Mass.: Newbury House.
———. 1972. "Differential Identity and the Social Base of Folklore." In *Towards New Perspectives in Folklore*, edited by Americo Paredes and Richard Bauman, 31–41. Austin: University of Texas Press.
Bauman, Richard, and Joel Sherzer, eds. 1986. *Story, Performance, and Event: Contextual Studies of Oral Narrative*. Cambridge, UK: Cambridge University Press.
———. 1974. *Explorations in the Ethnography of Speaking*. Cambridge, UK: Cambridge University Press.
Becker, Carl L. 1958. "What Are Historical Facts?" In *Detachment and the Writing of History: Essays and Letters of Carl Becker*, edited by Phil L. Snyder, 41–64. Ithaca: Cornell University Press.
Beckham, Stephen Dow. 2005. "Indian Claims Commission, 1946–78: A Brief History with Comments Relating to Docket 218." Unpublished report.
———. 1993. *Responses to Obvious Deficiency Review: Petition of the CIT*. Supplementary Petition Material. U.S. Bureau of American Ethnology: U.S. Department of the Interior.
———. 1991. *The Modern Cowlitz Community: Measures of Tribal Continuity and Identity*. Supplementary Petition Material. U.S. Bureau of American Ethnology: U.S. Department of the Interior.
———. 1986. "Repeated Identification by Federal Authorities States Counties Parishes Cities Anthropologists, Historian, Newspapers, and Other Tribes." Criterion 54. 7(a) (1)-(7) Lake Oswego, Ore.
Behar, Ruth. 1996. *The Vulnerable Observer*. Boston: Beacon Press.
Ben-Amos, Dan. 1972. "Toward a Definition of Folklore in Context." In *Toward New Perspectives in Folklore*, edited by Américo Paredes and Richard Bauman, 1–15. Austin: University of Texas Press.

———. 1967. "Folklore: The Definition Game Once Again." Paper delivered at the meeting of the American Folklore Society. Toronto, Ontario.
———, ed. 1976. *Folklore Genres*. Austin: University of Texas Press.
Bendix, Regina. 2000. "The Pleasures of the Ear: Toward an Ethnography of Listening." *Cultural Analysis* 1: 33–50.
———. 1990. "Reflections on Earthquake Narratives." *Western Folklore* 40: 331–47.
Benedict, Ruth. 1946. *The Chrysanthemum and the Sword: Patterns of Japanese Culture*. Boston: Houghton Mifflin.
———. 1934. *Patterns of Culture*. New York: Houghton Mifflin.
Benjamin, Walter. 1969a. "The Storyteller." In *Illuminations*, edited by Hannah Arendt, 69–82. New York: Schocken.
———. 1969b. "The Work of Art in the Age of Mechanical Reproduction." In *Illuminations*, edited by Hannah Arendt, 215–52. New York: Schocken.
Berkhofer, Robert. 1979. *The White Man's Indian: Images of the American Indian from Columbus to Present*. New York: Vintage.
Berman, Judith. 2004. "Some Mysterious Means of Fortune: A Look at North Pacific Coast Oral History." In *Coming to Shore: Northwest Coast Ethnology, Traditions*, edited by Michael E. Harkin and Sergei Kan, 129–62. Lincoln: University of Nebraska.
Bierhorst, John. 1985. *The Mythology of North America*. New York: Quill William Morrow.
Biolsi, Thomas. 1989. "The American Indian and the Problem of Culture: A Review of the American Indian and the Problem of History." *American Indian Quarterly* 13: 261–69.
Blanchet, Father. 1956. *Notices and Voyages of the Famed Quebec Mission to the Pacific Northwest*. Portland, Ore.: Champoeg Press.
Bloch, Maurice. 1996. "Internal and External Memory: Different Ways of Being in History." In *Tense Past: Cultural Essays in Trauma and Memory*, edited by P. Antze and M. Lambek, 215–33. London: Routledge.
Boas, Franz. 1975 [1909]. *The Kwakiutl of Vancouver Island*. Memoirs of the American Museum of Natural History, volume 8, part 2, 301–522. New York: American Museum of Natural History. Reprint, New York: American Philosophical Society.
———. 1970 [1916]. Tsimshian Mythology. *Thirty-First Annual Report of the United States Bureau of American Ethnology*. Washington, D.C.: U.S. Government Printing Office. Reprint, New York: Johnson.
———. 1940a. "The Aims of Anthropological Research." In *Race, Language, and Culture*, edited by Franz Boas, 243–59. New York: Macmillan.
———. 1940b. "The Aims of Ethnology." In *Race, Language, and Culture*, edited by Franz Boas, 626–38. New York: Macmillan.
———. 1940c. "The Limitation of the Comparative Method in Anthropology." In *Race, Language, and Culture*, edited by Franz Boas, 270–80. New York: Macmillan.
———, ed. 1940d. *Race, Language, and Culture*, New York: Macmillan.
———. 1955 [1927]. *Primitive Art*. Oslo: Instituttet for Sammenlignende Kulturforskning by H. Ascheoug, 1927. Cambridge: Harvard University Press. Reprint, New York: Dover Publications.
———. 1935. "Kwakiutl Tales." Columbia University Contributions to Anthropology, volume 26. 1910. New York: Columbia University Press.
———. 1932a. "Bella Bella Tales." *Memoirs of the American Folk-Lore Society* 25: 1–178.

———. 1932b. "Current Beliefs of the Kwakiutl Indians." *Journal of American Folklore* 45: 177–276.

———. 1930. *The Religion of the Kwakiutl Indians*, volumes 1 and 2. New York: Columbia University Press.

———. 1916. *Kathlamet Texts*. Bulletin 26. Washington, D.C.: U.S. Bureau of American Ethnology.

———. 1900. "The Mythology of the Bella Coola." Memoirs of the American Museum of Natural History.

———. 1895. "The Social Organization and Secret Societies of the Kwakiutl Indians." Report of the U.S. National Museum for 1895, 311–738.

———. 1894. *Chinook Texts*. Washington, D.C.: U.S. Government Printing Office.

———. 1888. "On Certain Songs and Dances of the Kwakiutl of British Columbia." *Journal of American Folklore* 1: 58–61.

Boldt, George (Boldt Decision). 1974. *United States v. Washington*, 384 F. Supp. 312 (W.D. Wash. 1974).

Bolduc, Jean Baptiste Zacharie. 1979. *Mission of the Columbia*. Fairfield, Wash.: Ye Galleon Press.

Bordewich, Fergus M. 1996. *Killing the White Man's Indian: Reinventing Native Americans at the End of the Twentieth Century*. New York: Doubleday.

Bouchard, Bob, and Julie Bouchard. 2003. Interview with author.

Bouchard, Jerry. 1997. Interview with the author. Longview, Wash.

Bourdieu, Pierre. 1977. *Outline of a Theory of Practice*. Cambridge, UK: Cambridge University Press.

Bowden, Henry W., and James P. Ronda, eds. 1980. "John Eliot's Indian Dialogues: A Study in Cultural Interaction." *Contributions in American History* 88: 3–56.

Boyd, Robert. 1999. *The Coming of the Spirit of Pestilence: Introduced Infectious Diseases and Population Decline among NW Coast Indians*. Seattle: University of Washington Press.

———, ed. 1999. *Indians, Fire, and the Land in the Pacific Northwest*. Corvallis: Oregon State University Press.

Braid, Donald. 1996. "Personal Narrative and Experiential Meaning." *Journal of American Folklore* 109, no. 431: 5–30.

Briggs, Charles. 1988. *Competence in Performance: The Creativity of Tradition in Mexican Verbal Art*. Philadelphia: University of Pennsylvania Press.

Burke, Kenneth. 1941. *The Philosophy of Literary Form*. Reprint, Berkeley: University of California Press.

Carbaugh, Donal. 1996. *Situation Selves: The Communication of Social Identities in American Scenes*. Albany: State University of New York Press.

Chomsky, Noam. 1968. *Language and Mind*. New York: Harcourt, Brace, Jovanovich.

Churchill, Ward. 1993. *Struggle for the Land*. Monroe, Maine: Common Courage Press.

———, ed. 2003. "Spiritual Hucksterism: The Rise of the Plastic Medicine Men." In *Shamanism: A Reader*, 324–33. London: Routledge.

Clifton, James. 1989. *Being and Becoming Indian*. Chicago: Dorsey Press.

Cohen, Felix S. 1942. *Handbook of Federal Indian Law*. Albuquerque: University of New Mexico Press.

Connerton, Paul. 1989. "Bodily Practice" In *How Societies Remember*. Cambridge, UK: Cambridge University Press.

Cook, Roy. 2003. "Indian Nations Tribal Sovereignty," pp. 1–3. Online at www.americanindiansource.com/sovereignty.html. Accessed on February 14, 2003.

Cook, Samuel R. 2002. "The Monacan Indian Nation Asserting Tribal Sovereignty in the Absence of Federal Recognition." *Wicazo Sa Review* (Fall): 91–116.

Cruikshank, Julie. 1998. "My Roots Grow in Jackpine Roots: Culture, History, and Narrative Practice in the Yukon." In *The Social Life of Stories: Narrative and Knowledge in the Yukon Territory*, 1–25. Lincoln: University of Nebraska Press.

———. 1995. Interviews with Angela Sidney, in "Pete's Song: Establishing Meanings through Story and Song." In *When Our Words Return: Writing, Hearing, and Remembering Oral Traditions of Alaska and the Yukon*, edited by Phyllis Morrow and William Schneider, 53–75. Logan: Utah State University Press.

———. 1994. "How the World Began [Tagish/Tlingit]." In *Coming to the Light: Contemporary Translations of the Native Myths of North America*, edited by Brian Swann, 138–51. New York: Random House.

———. 1992. "Claiming Legitimacy: Prophecy Narratives from Northern Aboriginal Women." *American Indian Quarterly* 18, no. 2: 3–22.

———. 1990. "On Oral History and Sense of Place: Getting the Words Right." *Arctic Anthropology* 27: 52–65.

Curtis, Edward. 1913. *The North American Indian: Being a Series of Volumes Picturing and Describing the Indians of the United States, the Dominion of Canada and Alaska*, edited by Frederick Webb Hodge, 9. Norwood, Mass.: Plimpton Press.

Daehnke, Jon. 2013. "We Honor the House": Lived Heritage, Memory, and Ambiguity at the Cathlapotle Plankhouse." *Wicazo Sa Review* 28, no. 1: 38–53.

———. 2010. "Reflections on the Confluence Project: Assimilation, Sustainability, and the Perils of Shared Heritage." *American Indian Quarterly* 36, no. 4: 503–14.

Darling, Nedra. 2002. *News from the U.S. Department of the Interior*. U.S. Department of Interior Bureau of Indian Affairs, Branch of Acknowledgment and Research.

Dauenhauer, Richard, and Nora Marks. 1996a. "Oral Literature Embodied and Disembodied." In *Talking on the Page: Editing Aboriginal Oral Texts. Papers Given at the Thirty-Second Annual Conference on Editorial Problems*, edited by Laura J. Murray and Keren Rice, 91–111. Toronto: University of Toronto Press.

———. 1996b. "Translating Text." In *Talking on the Page: Editing Aboriginal Oral Texts. Papers Given at the Thirty-Second Annual Conference on Editorial Problems*, edited by Laura J. Murray and Keren Rice, 5–42. Toronto: University of Toronto Press.

———. 1994a. "'Glacier Bay History' Told by Amy Marvin and 'Speech for the Removal of Grief' Delivered by Jessie Dalton [Tlingit]." In *Coming to the Light: Contemporary Translations of the Native Myths of North America*, edited by Brian Swann, 151–76. New York: Random House.

———. 1994b. *Haa Kusteeyí, Our Culture: Tlingit Life Stories*. Seattle: University of Washington Press.

———. 1990. *Haa Tuwunáagu Yís, for Healing Our Spirit*. Seattle: University of Washington Press.

———. 1987. *Haa Shuká / Our Ancestors: Tlingit Oral Narratives*. Seattle: University of Washington Press.

Davis, Mary B. 1994. "Cowlitz Indians." In *Native America in the Twentieth Century: An Encyclopedia*, edited by Michael Roe, 147–49. New York: Garland.

Debachere, M. C. 1995. "Problems in Obtaining Grey Literature." *IFLA Journal* (Inter-

national Federation of Library Associations and Institutions), 21, no. 2: 94–98.
De Certeau, Michel. 1984. *The Practice of Everyday Life*. Berkeley: University of California Press,.
Deer, Ada. 1997. "Mandatory Criteria per CFR 83. 7 (a)-(g) Federal Register, February 27, 1997." U.S. Department of Interior Bureau of Indian Affairs, Branch of Acknowledgment and Research.
Dundes, Alan. 1989. *Folklore Matters*. Knoxville: University of Tennessee Press.
———. 1964. "Texture, Text, and Context." *Southern Folklore Quarterly* 28: 251–65.
———. 1965. "What Is Folklore?" In *The Study of Folklore*, edited by Alan Dundes, 1–3. Englewood Cliff, N.J.: Prentice-Hall.
Duranti, Alessandro. 1992. "Oratory." In *Folklore, Cultural Performances, and Popular Entertainment*, edited by Richard Bauman, 154–56. New York: Oxford University Press.
Durkheim, Emile. 1982 [1895]. *Rules of Sociological Method*. Reprint, New York: Free Press.
Echohawk, John E. 2000. *Federal Recognition of Indian Tribes*. Native American Rights Fund. Online at http://216. 69. 166. 179/pubs/justice/2000fall.html. Accessed on February 14, 2003.
Federal Register. 1994. Volume 59 (February 25), p. 9,295.
Feintuch, Burt. 2001. "Longing for Community." *Western Folklore* (Spring): 149–61.
Field, Les. 2003. "Unacknowledged Tribes, Dangerous Knowledge." *Wicazo Sa Review* (Fall): 79–94.
Fitzpatrick, Darleen. 1986. "We Are Cowlitz." PhD diss. Seattle: University of Washington.
Foley, John Miles. 1992. "Word Power, Performance, and Tradition." *Journal of American Folklore* (Summer): 275–301.
Foucault, Michel. 1980. *Power/Knowledge and Other Selected Writings, 1972–1977*. New York: Pantheon.
———. 1977a. *Discipline and Punish: The Birth of the Prison*, translated by Alan Sheridan. New York: Pantheon Books.
———. 1977b. "Nietzsche, Genealogy, History." In *Language, Counter-Memory, Practice: Selected Essays and Interviews*, edited by Donald F. Bouchard, 136–39. Ithaca: Cornell University Press.
———. 1972. *The Archeology of Knowledge and Discourse on Language*. New York: Pantheon.
Franchere, Gabriel. 1854. *Narrative of the Voyage to the NW Coast of America in the Years 1811, 1812,1813, and 1814; or, The First American Settlement on the Pacific*. New York: Redfield.
Friday, Chris. 2008. "Performing Treaties: The Culture and Politics of Treaty Remembrance and Celebration." In *The Power of Promises*, edited by Alexandra Harmon, 157–83. Seattle: University of Washington Press.
Friedman, Jonathan. 1992. "The Past in the Future: History and the Politics of Identity." *American Anthropologist* 94 (December): 837–59.
Gallatin, Albert. 1848. "Hale's Indians of North-west America." *Transactions of the American Ethnological Society* 2: 1–130.
Garroutte, Eva Marie. 2003. *Real Indians: Identity and Survival of Native America*. Berkeley: UCLA Press.

Geertz, Clifford. 1973. "Thick Description: Toward an Interpretive Theory of Culture." In *The Interpretation of Cultures: Selected Essays by Clifford Geertz*, 3–30. New York: Basic Books.

Gibbs, George. 1967 [1855]. *Indian Tribes of the Washington Territory*. Reprint, Fairfield, Wash.: Galleon Press.

Glassie, Henry. 1991. *Turkish Traditional Art Today*. Bloomington: Indiana University Art Museum.

Goffman, Erving. 1974. *Frame Analysis*. Cambridge: Harvard University Press.

———. 1959. *The Presentation of Self in Everyday Life*. New York: Anchor Books Doubleday. Grant, Ulysses S. 1873. Statement of November 4, 1873. In *Indian Affairs Law and Treaties, Vol. 1*, compiled and edited by Charles J. Kappler. Washington, D.C.: U.S. Government Printing Office. Online at http://digital.library.okstate.edu/kappler/Vol1/HTML_files/WAS0901.html. Accessed on November 12, 2003.

Grim, John A. 1996. "Cultural Identity, Authenticity, and Community Survival: The Politics of Recognition in the Study of Native American Religion." *American Indian Quarterly* 20 (nos. 3–4): 353–76.

Gumperz, John, and Dell Hymes, eds. 1964. "The Ethnography of Communication." *American Anthropologist* 66, no. 6 part 2: 1–177.

Gunther, Erna. 1949. *The Shaker Religion of the Northwest*. Seattle: University of Washington Press.

———. 1940. *Ethnobotany of Western Washington: The Knowledge and Use of Indigenous Plants*. Seattle: University of Washington Press.

Haeberlin, Herman, and Erna Gunther. 1930. *The Indians of Puget Sound*. Seattle: University of Washington Press.

Haeberlin, Herman, and James A. Teit. 1928. "Coiled Basketry in BC and Surrounding Regions." 41st Annual Report of the BAE to the Secretary of the Smithsonian Institution, 1919–1924, pp. 133–42. Washington, D.C.: U.S. Government Printing Office.

Hajda, Yvonne. 1990. "Coast Salish." In *Handbook of North American Indians*, edited by Wayne Suttles, volume 7, pp. 512–15. Washington, D.C.: Smithsonian Institution Press.

Halbwachs, Maurice. 1992. *On Collective Memory*, edited by Lewis A. Coser. Heritage of Sociology Series, 254. Chicago: University of Chicago Press.

Hale, Horatio. 1846. "Synopsis and Vocabularies." In *Ethnography and Philology*, volume 6, pp. 570–629. Philadelphia: Lea and Blanchard.

Harkin, Michael E. 1997. *The Heiltsuks: Dialogues of Culture and History on the Northwest Coast*. Lincoln: University of Nebraska Press.

Harmon, Alexandra. 2008. *The Power of Promises*. Seattle: University of Washington Press.

———. 1998. *Indians in the Making*. Berkeley: University of California Press, 1998.

Haugbølle, Sune. 2003. "Looking the Beast in the Eye: Collective Memory and the Civil War in Lebanon." Online at http://www.111101.net/Writings/index.php?http://www.111101.net/Writings/Essays_Research/sune_haugbolle/sune_haugbolle_01.php. Accessed on October 23, 2003.

Heaney, Leo. 1984. "Cowlitz Petition for Recognition." Narrative.

Heidegger, Martin. 1971. "Building, Dwelling, Thinking." In *Poetry, Language, Thought*, translated by Albert Hofstadter, 89–139. New York: Harper Colophon Books.

Henson, C. L. 1996. "From War to Self Determination." *American Studies Today*. Liverpool Community College and the Contributors. Online at www.americansc.org.uk/Online/indians.htm. Accessed on September 5, 2006.

Hill, Randall T. G. 1997. "Methodological Approaches to Native American Narrative and the Role of Performance." *American Indian Quarterly* 21, no. 1: 111–47.

Hinsley, Curtis. 1981. *Savages and Scientists: The Smithsonian Institution and the Development of American Anthropology*. Washington, D.C.: Smithsonian Institution Press.

"History of St. Francis." 2005. *St. Francis Xavier Mission*. Online at www.toledotel.com/~stfrancis/page9.html. Accessed in 2005.

Hobsbawm, Eric, and Terence Ranger, eds. 1983. *The Invention of Tradition*. Cambridge, UK: Cambridge University Press.

Hughes, Jennifer. 2001. "Primer on Federal Recognition and Current Issues Affecting the Process." Prepared for National Congress of American Indians, Winter Session, February 22. Online at www.msaj.com/papers/FedRecPrimer.html. Accessed March 6, 2003.

Hunn, Eugene S. 2007. "Chapter 4: Review of Linguistic Information." In *Cultural Affiliation Report*. National Park Service, Archeology Program. Online at www.cr.nps.gov/archeology/kennewick/Hunn.htm.

———. 2000. "Kennewick Man: Review of Linguistic Information." U.S. Department of Interior National Park Service Archeology Cultural Affiliation Report, Chapter 4, February. Online at www.cr.nps.gov/archeology/kennewick/Hunn.htm. Accessed on March 13, 2003.

———. 1996. "Columbia Plateau Indian Place Names: What Can They Teach Us?" *Journal of Linguistic Anthropology* 6, no. 1: 3–26.

———. 1990. *Nch'i-Wana, The Big River: Mid-Columbia Indians and Their Land*. Seattle: University of Washington Press.

Hymes, Dell. 1992. "Use All There Is to Use." In *On the Translation of Native American Literatures*, edited by B. Swann, 83–124. Washington, D.C.: Smithsonian Institution Press.

———. 1985. "Language, Memory, and Selective Performance: Cultee's 'Salmon's Myth' as Twice Told to Boas." *Journal of American Folklore* 98, no. 390: 391–435.

———. 1981a. *In Vain I Tried to Tell You: Essays in Native American Ethnopoetics*. Philadelphia: University of Pennsylvania Press, 1981.

———. 1981b. "Sociolinguistic Theory in Anthropology." *International Journal of Sociology of Language* 31: 91–108.

———. 1980a. *Language in Ethnography Series Language in Education: Ethnolinguistic Essays*. Washington, D.C.: Center for Applied Linguistics.

———. 1980b. "Verse Analysis of a Wasco Text." *International Journal of American Linguistics* 46: 65–77.

———. 1975. "Breakthrough into Performance." In *Folklore: Performance and Communication*, edited by Dan Ben-Amos and Kenneth Goldstein, 12–74. The Hague: Mouton, 1975.

———. 1974. "Ways of Speaking." In *Explorations in the Ethnography of Speaking*, edited by Richard Bauman and Joel Sherzer, 433–52. New York: Cambridge University Press.

———. 1973. "An Ethnographic Perspective." *New Literary History* 5: 187–201.

———. 1971a. "Competence in Performance in Linguistic Theory." In *Language Acquisition: Models and Methods*, edited by Renira Huxley and Elisabeth Ingram, 3–28. London: Academic Press.

———. 1971b. "The Contribution of Folklore to Sociolinguistic Research." In *Toward New Perspectives in Folklore*, edited by Americo Paredes and Richard Bauman, 43–51. Austin: University of Texas Press.

———. 1970. "Linguistic Method in Ethnography." In *Method and Theory in Linguistics*, edited by Paul L. Garvin. Janua Linguarum. Series Maior, 40. The Hague: Mouton.

———. 1963. "Linguistic Method in Ethnography." *Studies in the History of Linguistics* 25: 135–213.

———. 1962. "The Ethnography of Speaking." In *Anthropology and Human Behavior*, edited by T. Gladwin, 13–53. Washington, D.C. : W. C. Sturtevant.

Hymes, Virginia. 2004. "'Celilo' as Told by Larry George (Upper Coquille Athapascan)." In *Voices from Four Directions: Contemporary Translations of the Native Literature of North America*, edited by Brian Swann, 195–209. Lincoln: University of Nebraska.

———. 1987. "Warm Springs Sahaptin Narrative Analysis, 1981." In *Native American Discourse, Poetics, and Rhetoric*, edited by Joel Sherzer and Anthony C. Woodbury, 62–102. Cambridge, UK: Cambridge University Press.

"Indian Reorganization Act." Online at www.factmonster.com/ce6/history/A0825118.html. Accessed on February 18, 2004.

Irwin, Judith. 1994. "The Dispossessed: The Cowlitz Tribe of Southwest Washington." Unpublished manuscript.

———. 1979. "The Cowlitz Way: A Round of Life." *Cowlitz Historical Quarterly* 21, no. 1: 5–24.

Irwin, Matthew. "Barre Toelken: Folklorist of Culture and Performance." Online at http://people.westminstercollege.edu/faculty/dstanley/folklore/Edited%20Final%20Draft/fiu10irwin.htm. Accessed on October 12, 2004.

Jacobs, Melville. 1966. "A Look Ahead in Oral Literature Research." *Journal of American Folklore* 79: 413–27.

———. 1960. *The People Are Coming Soon: Analysis of Clackamas Chinook Myths and Tales*. Seattle: University of Washington Press.

———. 1959. *The Content and Style of an Oral Literature: Clackamas Chinook Myths and Tales*. Chicago: University of Chicago Press.

———. 1934. *Northwest Sahaptin Texts*. Columbia University Contributions to Anthropology, volume 19, parts 1 and 1. New York: Columbia University Press.

Jacklet, Ben. 1997. "Back from Extinction." *The Stranger* 6, no. 33: 12–17.

Jamtgaard, Sharon. 1997–2005. Conversations with the author. Newport, Ore.

———. 2004. Interview with the author, pp. 1–3. Newport, Ore.

Kane, Paul. 1968 [1869]. *Wandering of an Artist among the Indians of North America*. Rutland, Vermont: Charles E. Tuttle and Co.

Kapchan, Deborah. 1996. "Performance." *Journal of American Folklore* 108: 478–508.

Kinkade, Dale M. 2004. *Cowlitz Dictionary and Grammatical Sketch*. University of Montana Occasional Papers in Linguistics no. 18. Missoula: University of Montana Publishing, 2004.

———. 1991. *Chehalis Dictionary*. University of Montana Occasional Papers in Linguistics no. 7. Missoula: University of Montana Publishing.

Kinton, Jack F. 1974. *Leaders in Anthropology: The Men and Women of the Science of Man.* Aurora: Social Science and Sociological Resources.
Krupat, Arnold. 1992a. *Ethnocriticism: Ethnography, History, Literature.* Berkeley: University of California Press.
———. 1992b. "On the Translation of Native American Song and Story." In *On the Translation of Native American Literatures,* edited by B. Swann. Washington, D.C.: Smithsonian Institution Press.
———. 1989. *The Voice in the Margin: Native American Literature and the Canon.* Berkeley: University of California Press.
———. 1983. "The Indian Autobiography: Origins, Type, and Function." In *Smoothing the Ground: Essays on Native American Oral Literature,* edited by Brian Swann, 23–42. Stanford: University of California Press.
Levi-Strauss, Claude, and Didier Eribon. 1991. *Conversations with Claude Levi-Strauss.* Chicago: University of Chicago Press.
Lomax, Alan. 1968. *Folk Song, Style, and Culture.* Washington, D.C.: Library of Congress Archives.
Lord, Albert. 1960. *The Singer of Tales.* Cambridge: Harvard University Press.
Lorenzo, June. 2004. "Summary of Land Rights in the U.S." Online at www.firstpeoples.org/land_rights/united_states/us_summary.htm. Accessed on June 3, 2004.
Magoulick, Mary. 2005. *Narratives.* Online at www.faculty.de.gcsu.edu/~mmagouli/narratives.htm. Accessed on November 11, 2005.
Matthews, P. H. 1997. "Ethnography of Speaking." In *The Concise Oxford Dictionary of Linguistics.* Oxford: Oxford University Press.
McCulloch, Anne M., and David E. Wilkins. 1995. "'Constructing' Nations within States: The Quest for Federal Recognition by the Catawba and Lumbee Tribes. *American Indian Quarterly* 19, no. 3: 361–68.
McDonald, Lucile. 1972. *Swan among the Indians: Life of James G. Swan, 1818–1900; Based upon Swan's Hitherto Unpublished Diaries and Journals.* Portland, Ore.: Binfords and Mort.
Meares, John. 1967 [1790]. *Voyages Made in the Years 1788 and 1789 from China to the NW Coast of America: With an Introductory Narrative of a Voyage Performed in 1786, from Bengal, in the Ship Nootka.* 2 vols. New York: Da Capo Press.
Meeker, Ezra. 1905. *Pioneer Reminiscences of the Puget Sound: The Tragedy of Leschi.* Seattle: Lowman and Hanford Stationary and Print.
Mills, Margaret. 1993. "Prismatic Personhood: Ethnographically Constructed Lives." *Papers in Comparative Studies* 8: 3–35.
Mooney, Frank. 1893. *Indian Doctors.* Frankfurt: Lunden Press.
Narayan, Kirin. 1993. "How Native Is a 'Native' Anthropologist?" *American Anthropologist* 95, no. 3: 671–86.
National Congress of American Indians Handbook. 1999. Online at www.ncai.org.
Native American Rights Fund (NARF). 2000. Online at www. narf.org.
Noyes, Dorothy. 1996. "Group." *Journal of American Folklore* 108: 499–78.
Okley, Judith, and Helen Callaway, eds. 1992. Preface. In *Anthropology and Autobiography.* Volume 29, pp. xi–1. London: ASA Monographs.
Olson, Mrs. Charles H. 1948. *Cowlitz County, Washington, 1854–1947.* Kelso, Wash.: Kelso Chamber of Commerce.

Paredes, Americo. 1993. "The Folklore of Groups of Mexican Origin in the United States." In *Folklore and Culture on the Texas-Mexican Border*, edited by Richard Bauman, 19–45. Austin: CMAS Books.

Paschal, Rachael. 1991. "The Imprimatur of Recognition: American Indian Tribes and the Federal Recognition Process." *Washington Law Review* 66, no. 1: 209–28.

Pevar, Stephen L. 1997. *The Rights of American Indians and Their Tribes: The Basic ACLU Guide to Indian and Tribal Rights (American Civil Liberties Union Handbook)*. Carbondale: Southern Illinois University Press.

Philips, Susan Urmston. 1983. *The Invisible Culture: Communication in the Classroom and Community on the Warm Springs Indian Reservation*. New York: Longman Press.

Pierce, Charles Sanders. 1965. *Collected Papers of Charles Sanders Peirce*, edited by Charles Hartshorne and Paul Weiss. Cambridge: Belknap Press of Harvard University.

Porth, Eric, Kimberley Neutzling, and Jessica Edwards. 2005. *Functionalism*. Online at www.as.ua.edu/ant/Faculty/murphy/function.htm. Accessed on January 16, 2004.

Ray, Verne. 1966. *Handbook of the Cowlitz Indians*. Seattle: Northwest Copy Company.

———. 1938. "Lower Chinook Ethnographic Notes." University of Washington Publications in Anthropology (Seattle) 7, no. 2: 29–165.

Rettig, James. 1986. "A Guide to the Indian Tribes of the Northwest." *Wilson Library Bulletin* 61: 80.

Rhodes, Justice. 2003. Interview with the author. Longview, Wash.

Richards, Kent D. 1979. *Isaac I. Stevens: Young Man in a Hurry*. Provo, Utah: Brigham Young University Press.

Ricoeur, Paul. 1979. "The Model of the Text: Meaningful Action Considered as a Text." In *Interpretive Social Science: A Reader*, edited by P. Rabinow and W. Sullivan, 92–123. Berkeley: University of California Press.

Roe, Michael. 2003. "Cowlitz Indian Ethnic Identity, Social Memories, and 150 Years of Conflict with the United States Government." In *The Role of Memory in Ethnic Conflict*, edited by Ed Cairns and Michael D. Roe, 55–73. New York: Palgrave Macmillan.

Roehrig, F. 1870. "Three Comparative Vocabularies of the Salish Language." Manuscript 3072. National Anthropological Archives, Smithsonian Institution, Washington, D.C.

Rubin, Gayle. 1975. "The Traffic of Women: Notes on the Political Economy of Sex." In *Toward an Anthropology of Women*, edited by Rayna R. Reiter, 157–210. New York: Monthly Review Press.

Ruby, Robert H., and John A. Brown, eds. 1981. *Indians of the Pacific Northwest: A History*. Norman: University of Oklahoma Press.

Sanchez-Carretero, Cristina. 1999. "Personal Narrative: A Cubist Perspective." Unpublished theoretical exam.

Sapir, E. 1907. "Preliminary Report on the Language and Mythology of the Upper Chinook. *American Anthropologist* 9: 533–44.

Scherzer, Joel, and Anthony C. Woodbury. 1987. *Native American Discourse: Poetics and Rhetoric*. New York: Cambridge University Press.

Schoenberg, Wilfred P. 1987. *A History of the Catholic Church in the Pacific Northwest: 1743–1983*. Washington, D.C.: Pastoral Press.

Seaburg, William R. 1981–82. "Guide to PACNW NA Materials in the Melville Jacobs Collection." HEA II-C Project. University Washington Libraries, Seattle.

Silverman, Carol. 1996. "Syllabus Introduction, 424/524 Feminist Methods in Anthropology." Unpublished. University of Oregon–Eugene.
Silverstein, Michael. 2003. "The When and Wheres—and Hows—of Ethnolinguistic Recognition." *Public Culture* 15, no. 3: 531–57.
Smith, Marian W. 1949. *Indians of the Urban Northwest*. New York: Columbia University Press.
Spier, Leslie. 1936. "Tribal Distribution in Washington." General Series in Anthropology. Coyote Press Facsimile Reprint.
Suttles, Wayne, ed. 1990. *Handbook of North American Indians*. Washington, D.C.: Smithsonian Institution Press.
Swan, James G. 1857. *The Northwest Coast*. New York: Harper Brothers.
Thom, Brian. 2006. "The Paradox of Boundaries." Paper presented at Cornell University Conference on Indigenous Cartographies and Representational Politics, Ithaca, N.Y., March 3–5.
———. 2005. "Coast Salish Senses of Place: Dwelling, Meaning, Power, Property, and Territory in the Coast Salish World." PhD diss., Department of Anthropology, McGill University, Montreal.
———. 2000. "Territory, Boundaries, and Overlapping Claims on the Northwest Coast." Paper presented at the 99th Annual Meeting of the American Anthropological Association. San Francisco, Calif., November 15–19.
Thompson, Courtenay. 2000. "Cowlitz Contested." *The Oregonian*, May 18.
Thwaites, Reuben G., ed. 1904–5. *Original Journals of the Lewis and Clark Expedition, 1804–1806*. 8 volumes. New York: Dodd, Mead,.
Titon, Jeff Todd. 1990. "The Life Story." *Journal of American Folklore* 93: 276–92.
Tobar-Dupres, Christine. 1998. "Northwest Coast." Unpublished topic paper. University of Pennsylvania.
Toelken, Barre. 2003. *The Anguish of Snails: Native American Folklore in the West*. Logan: Utah State University Press.
———. 1998. "The Yellowman Tapes." *Journal of American Folklore* 111: 442.
———. 1979. *The Dynamics of Folklore*. Boston: Houghton Mifflin.
———. 1969. "The Pretty Languages of Yellowman: Genre, Mode, and Texture in Navajo Coyote Narratives." *Genre* 2: 211–35.
Tolmie, William Fraser. 1963. *The Journals of William Fraser Tolmie, Physician and Fur Trader*. Vancouver, Canada: Mitchell Press.
Torner, Gary. 2004–5. Conversations and e-mails with the author.
Torner, Robin. 2003–5. Conversations and correspondence with the author.
———. 1994. "The Cowlitz Chronicles." Unpublished manuscript.
Treaty of Olympia. 1855. Online at http://nwifc.org/member-tribes/treaties/. 283 U. S. at 756–60, 51 S. Ct. at 615–17. Institution Treaty of Olympia, the Executive Order of November 4, 1873, and the 1911 Allotment Act. National Congress of American Indians Handbook, 1999. Online at www.ncai.org. Accessed on October 12, 2002.
Unger, Chelsea. 2006–7. Interview with author. Vancouver, Wash.
United States District Court for the District of Oregon. 1980. "Transcription of deposition of Verne F. Ray, March 27–28, 1980." In *The Wahkiakum Band of Chinook Indians, et al v. Mrs. Allen Bateman et al., volume ii: In Support of Plaintiff's Supplemental Memorandum in Opposition to Motions for Summary Judgment*.

U.S. Department of Interior, Bureau of Indian Affairs, Branch of Acknowledgement and Research. 1997. *The Official Guidelines to the Federal Acknowledgement Regulations*. 25 CFR 83 (Revised). Washington, D.C.: Government Printing Office.

U.S. General Accounting Office. 2001. "Indian Issues: Improvements Needed in Tribal Recognition Process. Report to Congressional Requesters." GAO-02-49. Washington, D.C.

Vizenor, Gerald. 1996. *Manifest Manners: Post Indian Warriors of Survivance*. Hanover, N.H.: University Press of New England.

Wagar, Michael. 2005. *Mount Saint Helens: Day of Fate*. Chehalis, Wash.: The Chronicle.

Wallace, Anthony F. C. 1972. *The Death and the Rebirth of the Seneca*. New York: Vintage.

Wallace, Pamela S. 2002. "Indian Claims Commission: Political Complexity and Contrasting Concepts of Identity." *Ethnohistory* 49, no. 4: 743–68.

Warbass, U. 1858. *George Gibbs Correspondence: Warbass to Gibbs. Cowlitz Landing, February 14, 1858*. Manuscript 726. National Anthropological Archives, Smithsonian Institution, Washington, D.C.

Weibel-Orlando, Joan. 1991. *Indian Country, L.A.: Maintaining Ethnic Community in a Complex Society*. Chicago: University of Illinois Press.

Wiget, Andrew. 1985. "Native American Oral Narrative." In *Native American Literature*. Boston: Twayne.

Wilkinson, Charles F. 2005. *Blood Struggle: The Rise of Modern Indian Nations*. New York: Norton.

Williams, Raymond. 1976. *Keywords: A Vocabulary of Culture and Society*. New York: Oxford University Press.

Wilson, Roy. 2000. *Medicine Circles*. Self-published. Toledo, Wash.

———. 1998. *Legends of the Cowlitz Indian Tribe*. Longview, Wash.: Express Press.

———. 1997a. *History of the Cowlitz Indian Tribe*. Self-published. Longview, Wash.

———. 1997b and 2003. Interviews with the author. Longview, Wash.

Wilson, Scott. 2006–7. Interviews with the author. Newport, Ore.

Zumwalt, Rosemary. 1988. *American Folklore Scholarship: A Dialogue of Dissent*. Bloomington: University of Indiana Press.

www.ingramcontent.com/pod-product-compliance
Lightning Source LLC
Chambersburg PA
CBHW030656230426
43665CB00011B/1119